THE SOPHISTICATE'S GUIDE TO LIVING ALONE SUCCESSFULLY

THE SOPHISTICATE'S GUIDE TO LIVING ALONE SUCCESSFULLY

RULE #1:
DON'T EAT OVER THE SINK...

EDAN SCHAPPERT

BETTERWAY PUBLICATIONS, INC.
WHITE HALL, VIRGINIA

Published by Betterway Publications, Inc.
Box 219
Crozet, VA 22932

Cover design by Deborah B. Chappell
Cover and text drawings by Donald Reilly

Library of Congress Cataloging in Publication Data

Schappert, Edan
    Sophisticate's guide to living alone successfully.

    Includes index.
    1. Single people—United States—Life skills guide.
I. Title.
HQ800.4.U6S32 1988   305'.90652   88-19377
ISBN 1-55870-107-9 (pbk.)

Printed in the United States of America
987654321

*To all the people in the world
who make music and bring joy
to the rafters of my one-person household.*

Acknowledgments

My thanks go out to all my friends on the West and East coasts who agreed with me enthusiastically that the time had come to write about the ups and downs of living alone.

And thanks especially to my writer friends, Patricia Schilbe and Shaaron Barish, and to Susan Bellows, who helped immensely with analyses of the manuscript.

And to Blanket, the cat on the about the author page, who nursed me through many a night's typing. (She thinks I'm a person who comes attached to a machine that makes clicking noises.) Her soft ears ready for cuddling, her purring, and her affectionate looks did a lot to help get this book written to meet a deadline.

And to Frank Sinatra's music that inspired me through many a gritty sit-down at the typewriter. Tape after tape of his would go into the recorder, and I'd feel surrounded by warmth.

And to everyone out there in the world with a sense of humor. You're my kind of person...and I think we're gaining.

E. S.
New York City

Foreword

You're divorced, widowed, single, or your spouse or significant other is in Europe for the next six months — and you are LIVING ALONE. There is no human being, by any figment of any imagination, living in your house or apartment with you. One person, one household. That's the story.

And how do you feel about it?

Whether your emotions range from "love it" to "can't stand it," it seems to be a fact of life at the current time.

If you're having qualms about this lifestyle, fear no more. Help is on the way. This book is going to tell you how to turn your life into a banquet.

You might be saying to yourself, "I just don't like it. I come home and there's no noise." So what are you going to do? Turn on that 24-hour news station, turn it up high, and get a blasting earful of what's going on in your town, city, country and the world. After 20 minutes of that (while stripping off your clothes and getting into something extra-comfortable to wear) you have overcome the deadly quiet of coming into a place with nobody there. Now you're ready to put on your favorite talk show or music station, tapes, or records. Your place now sounds like a lived-in warm place, and you're ready to tackle Project X, even if it's just taking a short nap to recover from all the world news you heard.

Or else you might be thinking, "Everyone feels sorry for me because I live alone." Well, you can unsorry those everyones in short order by starting to do *everything* you've ever wanted to do. You've got the chance of a lifetime to do things for yourself and others that you never would have time for if you were living with someone else. (Although it's unquestionably sensational having a housemate, sharing your space with a live-in person does take time and energy.)

This thought also may occur to you; "I'm used to having someone do things for me. I don't want to be self-sufficient. I don't know how to (a) balance a checkbook; (b) cook; (c) shop for groceries. Not only will you, of necessity, learn to do these things, you'll find there's a certain amount of creative satisfaction in completing tasks you thought were out of your realm.

You may say, in your early and anxious days, "Burglars will get me, goblins will come down the chimney and scare me, and what's that noise I hear in the kitchen?" But week after week and month after month will go by and you'll find these bogeyman fears do not materialize to "do you in." You relax and enjoy your home, just as you did when you had a housemate or mates.

There may be many other things spinning in your head if you're a first-time live-aloner, but most can be turned around to your advantage: "I have no one." Well, who are those relatives and friends of yours? They're not no-ones, they've been there for you before you lived alone and they are there now. Even though you live alone, you're not alone. And the telephone was invented so you can phone them up and make great plans with them. "I'll never fill all the time I have." Don't say that. The world is your oyster and you should start nibbling all the good things that await you— any of the things *you* choose. You know the other things you've thought of as you live alone, but as you read this book, you'll find a way through the maze, the mist will clear, and you'll say, "Why didn't someone tell me about these things before?"

You have a wonderful lifestyle ahead of you, much like the millions of others who enjoy living alone. So, come on along with us and have a great time. Things are looking up.

Contents

1

Living Alone.
A Bowl of Cherries?
Or the Pits

We all know what living alone is. It's a lack of patter of any other feet around the house.

The U.S. Census Bureau refers to us as "one-person house-holders."

If we find ourselves living alone for whatever reason or circumstance, we can take the situation and turn it into a *very* successful experience.

All we have to do is find out how.

Books have been written on the fluff side of living alone: how to redecorate your apartment or house, what to buy in the way of VCRs, jacuzzis, and high-tech potholders, and how to serve a romantic midnight snack — with accompanying menu and photo of candlelit table.

But we're going into the guts of the issue: HOW TO MAKE LIVING ALONE A REAL SUCCESS.

You'll find out how to throw out the things that don't tick in your life and keep the things that do; all while adding pizzazz to your day. We'll define anything that's warm, satisfying, rib-tickling, pleasurable, productive, expansive, happy, outgoing, and giving, as pizzazz.

The idea of being a sophisticated person living solo is that you don't let your life go down in the dumps just because you're alone. It's the easiest thing to let life get bleak and bleary, but that's not what we want. We want the opposite: a life that's lived with class and style, at least eighty percent of the time.

People living by themselves, of course, get lonely once in a while. (Who doesn't get lonely once in a while?) But the main point is that people in this lifestyle have a lot going for them which allows them to turn their lives around in very meaningful ways.

What's waiting for you around the corner will definitely please you.

Those of us living in one-person households are in all economic levels and ages (from eighteen to 118). We're living everywhere on the face of the globe — in houses, apartments, houseboats, tents, and treehouses.

A variety of situations make a one-person household. Some of us are divorced, some of us are widows or widowers, and some of us are single people winging it on our own.

It's really kind of a swanky way to live, and there can be a lot of joie de vivre in our lifestyle.

As a person living alone, however, there's one blunt fact to be faced. No matter what other luxuries we may have, there is no shoulder six inches away to depend on, fall on, or cry on. Most of us do have a shoulder to call on somewhere out there, but it takes time for the shoulder to come to the house when it's needed — or for us to go out of the house and travel to that shoulder.

We also have to be our own main motivators. There's no one at our elbows spurring us on and bringing us tea and crumpets or martinis and olives to keep our spirits up as we go through the interesting and not-so-interesting twists and turns of life.

In 1985, according to the Bureau of the Census (Series P-20, No. 402), there were 20,602,000 of us living in one-person households. In 1986 the figure increased to 21,178,000, over half a million people in one year.

If you're facing the prospect of living by yourself for the first time, you may be feeling panicky. This will easily be changed when you find out all the new things waiting for you — especially gifts of time, energy, and freedom to plot and carry out some great ideas.

There are a few requirements that must be met as you launch off into the glamorous solo life. Mainly, you must not let yourself and the stuff around you get too messy. This is important. You must be a bit debonair while living this lifestyle. Eating over the sink is *so* easy for the one-person householder, but we're going to try not to do it (too often).

Another requirement is: be the kind of person other people want to be with. You don't want to be "that poor soul who lives alone," but, "That terrific person who seems to be really getting something out of life.

I've been living alone for a number of adventurous years, and I've tried both "unsophisticated" (unhappy, a mess, few laughs, broke, and uncharming) and sophisticated (fairly happy, pulled together, non-broke, semi-charming, and breaking out into real laughs a minimum of eleven times a day). Sophisticated works better.

When we think about it, there seem to be several basic types of living arrangements in the world.

BASIC LIVING ARRANGEMENTS IN THE WORLD

1. A Terrific Marriage or Relationship
2. A Just-OK Marriage or Relationship
3. A Terrible Marriage or Relationship
4. Living Alone in a Terrific Way
5. Living Alone in a Just-OK Way
6. Living Alone in a Terrible Way

(Family and group living would be included in numbers 1, 2, and 3.)

If for some reason you don't have the number one choice, "A Terrific Marriage or Relationship," which would you choose?

I've chosen category 4, "Living Alone in a Terrific Way."

As a point of interest, by not slipping into a Just-OK or Terrible Marriage, I've so far saved the country six statistics:

● One murder
● Five divorces

In my mind, the top living arrangement is the terrific marriage or relationship. I'm sure you've noticed people in this category. There's usually a feeling that flows around these couples: they adore each other through thick and thin, and there's no make-believe about it, it just is. My favorite pair is from a 1940's black-and-white movie, "Mrs. Miniver." Did Greer Garson and Walter Pidgeon love each other, or what? Try to see this movie whenever it comes on TV.

But I'm in the second choice category, "Living Alone in a Terrific Way."

Living this way takes effort, imagination, and creativity, but the payoffs are high. And don't forget, there's no saying that a Terrific Marriage or Relationship might not be waiting in the wings and may happen when you least expect it. (We have lots of things to anticipate in our category of living.)

Here's a sampling of some of the good things you'll experience while living alone.

GOOD THINGS THAT HAPPEN WHEN YOU LIVE ALONE

- You can come and go as you like.
- You can have company when you want it, and no company when you don't want it.
- You can let the bathroom get messy.
- You can stay up until 4 A.M. watching old movies to your heart's content.
- All the bathroom shelves, dresser drawers, and closets are for YOUR things, and you can let them get cluttered.
- You can make funny noises of any kind at any time.
- You have time to do a lot of things for other people.
- You have total control over your financial situation.
- You never have to be "on stage." You can be yourself.
- You are the key participant, judge, and jury of your life. In your household, the spotlight is on you.

Naturally, there are pits in this lifestyle, too.

We have no one there 100 percent of the time to listen to 1) our good news and 2) our grouches and ouches.

Once some of my writing material was accepted by the Public Broadcasting Corporation for production. I was elated to come home at the end of the day and open up an envelope with this good news. I raced to the phone and called friends to tell them, but no one was home. This was a definite example of the pits of living alone.

I finally got hold of all of them several hours later, but the exquisite first blush of success was not there.

Here's a list of some of our other pits.

THE PITS IN LIVING ALONE

- It's quiet.
- *You* have to take out all the garbage.
- When your friends and relatives are out of town and you want someone to talk to — you're stuck. All you have left to talk with is

the cat.

● Emergencies must be kept to a minimum, because there's no one right there to come to your rescue.

But more of the pizzazz (eighty percent) and the pits (twenty percent) later. For now, we can say that a person living alone goes through lots of peaks and valleys, but who doesn't.

The one element of living alone that takes precedence over any other, however, is that you have *luxuries* that no other lifestyle has. They alone are worth the pits we have.

2

Your Money.
A Cash Flow...
Or a Cash Drip

Before sophisticated people living by themselves can have their wits about them, they must have money coming in.

There were a few times in my adventurous single-householder life when my Cash Flow dried up to a Cash Drip. This was not good.

We worry when no or little money is coming in. Not only that, people call us on the telephone asking for money for electricity bills and Visa cards that are due. And these people have taken classes to be cranky. They are trained to take us out of the worry state about money and put us into the wild-eyed fear state.

Sophisticated one-person householders do not want to look wild-eyed and fearful. That is why finances must be in order.

How can you tell if your finances are in order? You can tell because there's an absence of money problems nipping at your heels. And the Wolf is Not At The Door. When the Wolf Is At The Door, you'll know it. You wake up at four o'clock in the morning and you stare at the eerie dimly-lit walls and you sweat and you wonder where you're going to get money. Then at 8:00 A.M. your phone rings and someone who is very rude is telling you they definitely want money that is past due. This is clearly an awful way to start the day.

You must get pressing money matters off your mind. Financial pressures make dents on our brains. Then our brains go down in the dumps and we start doing strange things.

There a few ways you can be in a non-pressured state about money.

First of all, you may be financially well off. You don't have to hold down a poor, mediocre, or even a wonderful job anywhere in a factory or corporate structure. This is called Having a Lot of

Money. Maybe you've been lucky — maybe you live off an inheritance, or you won the lottery, or you're making money willy-nilly and it's coming in at breakneck speed.

I know someone in the Having a Lot of Money category. He is fairly young, and he moans and groans about how he can't make ends meet. Knowing he is wealthy with homes in New York and Texas, I asked him what the problem was. He said he can't live on the $200,000 (that's TWO HUNDRED THOUSAND DOLLARS) per year that — get this — INTEREST ON HIS ESTATE provides him. He has to really pinch pennies to live on the mere $200,000. Boo hoo. I commiserate with him. How sad.

The man is definitely in the financially independent category and doesn't have to work (which he doesn't).

But back to the rest of us. We must gather our wits and our abilities about us and figure out a way to get money coming in. Most times this has something to do with a paycheck.

I know a woman living alone at age eighty-two who likes the idea of a paycheck coming in. She goes out and does what she calls "Sitting with Old People." It's her part-time job several times a week. She finds people who need extra care or companionship, drives over to their places, makes meals, talks and laughs about various things with them, then goes home and gets weekly paychecks from the hourly rate she charges. She's put pizzazz in her life.

Someone with a small income can live alone and have a life that's got pep. It's easier being a one-person householder with a lot of money, but it's easier being *anything* with a lot of money.

We all need to have some kind of steady check or paycheck coming in. For a person living solo, there is no question about this.

It seems that companies, corporations, factories, and government agencies — while they may not be the best places to go in the dawn's early light each day— absolutely do have paychecks inside their buildings. The best way to get paychecks is to go into their buildings and work. The companies won't mail you their paychecks. You have to go and do something for them —inside their buildings — in order to get their paychecks.

In my experience, I've found it's better to get a little bit frazzled by going to work five days or so a week than to be a lot frazzled having no money at all coming in.

This is not to say we snap our fingers and get the ultimate peak experience of a job. But doing *something* is better than any kind of long term unemployment. Unemployment is frazzled living in the ultimate. Unemployment makes one feel haunted.

Someone I met once was complaining to me about not having much money coming in — year after year — and added, "But I would never take a job, whether I could get one or not. Working makes people so gray and dreary!"

Twelve hours later I thought of a response: "Yes, but LACK OF MONEY makes people even grayer!" To my dismay, I didn't have the chance to tell the person this zingy response.

The person who made the "work-makes-one-dreary" remark, by the way, jittered, had trembling fingers, was gray-looking, had tics in the face, and was generally falling apart at the seams. The person taught me a lesson.

Clearly, before anything else, we have to get our bucks in order. Money-pinching is just as bad as shoe-pinching. It shows on your face. And you can't get a snazzy, productive, and somewhat smile-filled life until you get settled down about money. You must have it coming in regularly.

The Number 1 choice is that you're rich.

Another choice is a high-paying job, and then, lower on the scale, a medium or low-paying job, or *some* activity that brings in bucks somehow.

To get more income, you might:
- Go back to school to get a degree to get you a better job.
- Teach others something you know about.
- Do a financial analysis about how to invest wisely.
- Produce an item you make very well, and sell a lot of it to people who can really use it.
- Work at getting promoted from whatever job you're in now.

Financial freedom involves a lot of self-help. Finding out about your talents and interests that can make a contribution to the world — and pay you amazingly well at the same time — is the route to financial happiness.

But the only way to do it is to do it. The age-old saying, Doing Beats Stewing, still applies.

So do something about your financial life.

Spend time researching and find *some* way of getting money pumping healthily towards you.

Then you'll go on with the real adventure of that sophisticated person living alone successfully.

3

Your Time of Your Life

Ever since time began, twenty-four hours a day times seven days a week is 168 hours.

Each person gets 168 hours a week.

It's what you put into those 168 hours that's important. We're all used to Chores and Errands and "I-have-to-do-this-and-that," but we also want to use time for totally productive hours and doing things we enjoy.

We know, by instinct, experience and just plain every other thing that buzzes at us, that we will spend much of our time earning our livelihood. We've covered that.

So let's glance down a mythical time chart, starting with 168 hours a week, and see where we spend from the Time Bank that we have.

The chart shows hypothetical hours; your chart could vary in every case.

Estimate how you spend your own weekly hours on the right-hand side of the chart. It's a real eye-opener as to where your time is spent.

You want (and can have) lots of time now for doing things you've always wanted to do that are productive and soul-enriching for you and other people. For example:
- If you don't know how to dance, go out and learn to dance, then go dancing.
- Take a course in anything you've always wanted to do.
- Read a book. Read three books. Read books to other people.
- Tutor kids.
- Visit someone who's laid up with an ailment.

- Organize to raise money for your favorite groups.
- Watch your favorite sports.
- Play your favorite sports.
- Learn to ice skate, learn to play tennis.
- Shop for fantastic clothes.
- Get your finances in order and get more money coming in.
- Study investments.
- Take a course. Take more courses. Get a degree.
- Learn to do anything new.
- Build something.
- Remodel a room.
- Remodel yourself.
- Go into politics.
- Organize a community, state, or national project.
- Figure out computers once and for all.
- Lose ten pounds and buy a new bathing suit.
- Go to a seminar.
- Go on a cruise.
- Buy real estate.
- Get a massage.
- Give a massage.
- Make a list of things you'd like to accomplish.
- Take a nap from exhaustion due to above item.
- Visit friends, solve small and big problems, laugh a lot.
- Visit relatives.
- Write your senators. Really let them have it.
- Write a Letter-to-the-Editor. Get mad.
- Read books to find your full potential and the ways to make your life a banquet.
- Rent a car. Take a trip.
- Buy a car. Take a longer trip.
- Write a book.

Look at it this way. When you're living along, your time is YOUR time. How many periods in our lives do we have this given to us? In school, our time is spent on getting things out of books, running them through our brains, and giving them back to a teacher. All well and good and necessary.

If we're living in a group or family unit, as loving and wonderful as it is, demands on your time are made — and you give your time gladly. But, IF you are living alone for whatever reason, you'll soon find that time is not against you, but your best friend.

And what about your time spent with friends?

The rule is: "I want to spend time with people who are fun, funny, or in some other way helpful and nurturing to me and me to them."

If for some reason you absolutely have to spend time with someone who doesn't laugh, is grumpy, or who does something to put you down or to make you feel bad, I guess you just have to do it. But keep it to a minimum. And try to learn a Teflon-persona, where the grumpy person's zings and barbs towards you don't stick to you.

You'll know something is wrong when you're with a grump, because your body reacts. Your face muscles used for laughing are going unused. Your face gets stiff. Your bottom that's sitting on the chair gets numb. Your eyes get glazed and hot and they start to feel wobbly.

Sometimes your teeth begin to itch. It's very odd to have teeth that itch. This is not a good way to spend time.

So to spare yourself all of this, gravitate towards people who find things to laugh about— especially themselves and the comical twists and turns of just going through a day.

Humor is known to have magical properties, as scientists are finding out. Laughter propels a chemical to squirt through our vital zones and, somehow, helps to keep our bodies healthy.

Enough about the laughing business. Simply fill some of your great non-duty, non-chore hours with laughing and holding your sides, as well as other people's sides.

Don't be phony about this laughing business, it's not "a job," it just happens, and it's a great way to spend time.

We can see that a person living solo gets a great big present: LOTS OF TIME. And when we have a game plan (see Time Chart that follows), we can fill it up with all the goodies we want.

Time is not hanging on your hands, it's begging you: "Take me! I'm yours!" What a gift.

Photocopy and fill out the chart with things you'd like to do. (Even if you do half of them, you're ahead of the game.) Photocopy a supply of the chart, and use them weekly.

A lot of the hours will be chalked out by 9 to 5's and necessities, but your remaining hours are totally yours. The sample, filled-out, page will give you an idea.

Time: It's all there for you, the one-person householder, to use in whatever way suits *you.*

Drawing by D. Reilly; © 1988 The New Yorker Magazine, Inc.

168 HOURS A WEEK GIVEN TO YOU

YOU START WITH 168 HOURS:	Hypothetical 168 Total Hours	Estimate How You Spend 168 Weekly Hours
● Minus 12 hours a day at the **job** × 5 days = YOU'RE LEFT WITH:	60 108 Hours	
● Minus 8 hours a night **sleeping** × 7 nights = YOU'RE LEFT WITH:	56 52 Hours	
● Minus 4 hours a week of **necessity shopping** = YOU'RE LEFT WITH:	4 48 Hours	
● Minus 3 hours a day for **eating** meals × 7 days = YOU'RE LEFT WITH:	21 27 Hours	
● Minus 3 hours a week **housekeeping duties** = YOU'RE LEFT WITH:	3 24 Hours	
● Minus 2 hours a week lugging **laundry** = YOU'RE LEFT WITH:	2 22 Hours	
● Minus 7 hours a week of **duties specific to your life** = YOU'RE LEFT WITH:	7 15 Hours Leisure Left In A Week For You	
● Minus 2½ hours of **leisure on** each weekend day, × 2 **weekend days** = YOU'RE LEFT WITH:	5 10 Hours	
● Minus 2 hours of **leisure on each weekday**, × 5 weekdays = **HOURS LEFT TO USE** =	10 0	

TIME CHART

	SUNDAY	MONDAY	TUESDAY	WEDNESDAY	THURSDAY	FRIDAY	SATURDAY
6:00 a.m.							
7:00 a.m.							
8:00 a.m.							
9:00 a.m.							
10:00 a.m.							
11:00 a.m.							
12:00 a.m.							
1:00 p.m.							
2:00 p.m.							
3:00 p.m.							
4:00 p.m.							
5:00 p.m.							
6:00 p.m.							
7:00 p.m.							
8:00 p.m.							
9:00 p.m.							
10:00 p.m.							
11:00 p.m.							
12:00 m							

4

Household Chores.
Reduce Them to
Almost Zero

Before going any further, we have to talk about three things:
1. Housecleaning the place where we live.
2. Buying supplies for the place where we live.
3. Washing sheets and towels that are used at the place where we live — called lugging laundry.

First, you must keep the place where you live somewhat clean and tidy. For instance, you must keep any miscellaneous toenail clippings and used toothpicks off of tables near where company might sit. You can get by with having your place in a shambles when company isn't coming over, but when company is on the way and they think you're a terrific, with-it, interesting, and on-top-of-it type person, you've got to get your mess in order.

Another example: Throw away that garbage bag under your kitchen sink where last night you put the peeled skin of a great big onion. Your kitchen and your house smells like a bad, aging onion after you peeled the onion one night and then left the peelings and miscellaneous bits of onion sit the next day in your garbage under your kitchen sink. You might be used to the fetid aroma in your place, but your company is not used to knock-out smells when visiting other people. One of the first rules of a sophisticated person living alone is this: try not to do anything that makes you or your house smell odd.

So remember to get your living quarters clean. Get your kitchen clean, the garbage out, and the bathroom clean, especially all kinds of fuzz and curlicues that automatically multiply on the bathroom floor when you're not home.

Get on your hands and knees and use a mini-vacuum, but remove fuzz and little curlicues and unidentified blobs off the bathroom floor.

Get the place looking like a non-deranged person lives there. You are a non-deranged person, but when people aren't living with you twenty-four hours a day, it's easy to let things get uncivilized, uncouth, and downright sloppy.

If you're a punk rock person who is making three million dollars a minute and you like living sloppy because it's part of your persona, then all these words of wisdom about onion peelings and blobs on the bathroom floor won't be important to you. But for the other ninety-nine percent of us in the world, we need to live in a clean and semi-sane habitat.

We especially need sanity around us so we can figure how to make enough money to *hire* someone else to clean our place.

Cleaning isn't really what a person living alone should be doing. We should be out doing fascinating things instead of home in the bathroom on our hands and knees flailing around with a Dustbuster.

Now another big item which piles up is laundry. Don't THINK about doing the laundry, just do it.

Pack it up, get the laundry detergent box or bottle you bought at the supermarket, go to the washer, wherever it is, get a juicy and trashy novel to read, put the laundry in the washer, read the trashy novel, take the stuff out of the washer and put it in the dryer, read the novel again, take the stuff out of the dryer and fold it fast.

Under no circumstances should you let laundry get you down. It must be done without angst. But it must be done. It's a well-known fact that when laundry isn't done, we find there are no sheets left to sleep on and there are no towels in the bathroom and we don't even have clean socks. Dirty laundry is not sophisticated.

So get in the habit of either doing the laundry or bringing it someplace where people will put it in the machines for you. In the latter case, you will get a ticket and you'll have to remember to go back to the laundry two days later with your ticket to get your sheets back.

After handling the laundry problem, go on doing what you should be doing: exploring the good things of life or taking a nap to refresh yourself for your next sashay out of the house.

Now, four more hours are going to have to be spent bringing supplies into the house. This is called shopping. This is a killer category.

Shopping errands can take over your life if you let them get the upper hand. An errand will nag you, "I need to be done, now!" Then another errand will say the same thing, then another and another. Whap them all down into a manageable and minimal time frame. A person living alone doesn't want to spend ninety percent of free time dealing with "things you have to get."

We know, however, that all sorts of dribs and drabs have to be brought into the house weekly to keep life going. And if you have a car, you have to constantly put dribs and drabs in that, too. But we want to spend only four (4!) hours in any kind of place where you get the necessities of life: supermarkets, gas stations, 7-11's, dry cleaners, and drugstores.

There are other stores that are considered pleasurable and we don't include them in the above category: Mercedes-Benz stores, shops and garden stores that sell flowers and lush plants, stores where they sell clothes that make you feel great, or any store that sells stuff that delights you or another person. These are called luxurious store visits.

Back to necessity shopping; there is the part called Grocery Shopping. We must do this week after week. Pretty soon you get tired of Grocery Shopping, so you'll want to reduce it as much as possible in your life. You definitely don't want to be a supermarket-dawdler.

Once you break the habit of supermarket-dawdling, you'll get a new lease on life. You'll be free. You'll feel like a person with an objective: your objective is to have a creative existence, not go around in circles at the supermarket concentrating on Comet Cleanser and Mop 'n Glo.

If, however, it is a genuine joy to you to take the time and energy to examine each can for price differentials and ounces included for the purpose of saving two or ten cents, then by all means do it. But try to think that it may be taking fifteen minutes to save the two cents, and you might use that fifteen minutes more productively and go for the *big* ideas in improving your own or others' circumstances. Living solo is the time to put wings on your thoughts — and to forget about two-cent projects and spending lots of time in supermarkets.

After a lot of fine-honing, I now do a week's shopping for groceries in a flat thirty-two minutes from the automatic "In" door to the automatic "Out" door. This cutting down on time is important. There's nothing glamorous in that supermarket. Your mind can move on to other things.

Of course, at times due to your efficiency, you'll get your groceries home and find you've plucked off the shelf a can of steamed clams when what you wanted was a can of ham and beans, or fattening mayonnaise instead of low-cal. Getting a few groceries by mistake is insignificant.

Let's go into some of the ways you can get time reduced at the supermarket:

1. Get your eye trained to spot an empty cart fast.
2. Reject a cart immediately if it veers in the wrong direction or if one of its wheels won't roll but just skids sideways on the floor. This cart will make you feel crazy.
3. Have your aisles memorized.
4. Keep walking as fast as possible as you push your cart and put things in it. Go around all the other people. Do not bump into the backs of the shoes of the other people in front of you. People don't like that.
5. Buy pretty much the same things every week that you know you're going to eat or use in the way of paper products or detergents. Simplify by buying all-white kitchen paper towels, paper napkins, toilet tissue, and facial tissue. Not only will you not have to stand at the displays picking out colors and onion and herb motifs, you'll be helping the environment by not putting dyes back into the water system.(The less dyes that reenter the environment, the better.) Unless you're planning a company dinner that week, don't pick up fancy things. If you buy fancy things, you'll eat them, which puts on pounds you don't want. BUY THE BASICS AND GET OUT OF THE STORE AND PUT THE GROCERIES IN YOUR CUPBOARDS AND FORGET ABOUT IT. Do not use supermarkets for entertainment. You'll have plenty of entertainment and fancy things at restaurants or at great dinners at other people's houses when you're invited for dinner. (And you'll be invited out a lot, because you're rested and charming and you have energy left to be fairly witty.)
6. Make a quick survey as you near the checkout stand. Let your senses tell you which is going to be the fast line.
Clue #1: A person ahead of you with his or her cart loaded on top and bottom with a three-week supply of household and food items is not going to make a fast line.
Clue #2: Someone who is holding a check with no endorsement stamped on the back is going to make a slow line. This person will

have to go to the Customer Service Department after all the items have been rung up, and the line will not move.

Clue #3: Someone, for some reason or another, crashes in line ahead of you and looks mean. Let him or her crash and just find another line. Don't argue with that person, no matter how many Assertiveness books you've read. Going "at it" with a supermarket line-crasher is a terrible waste of time. You don't want to have a seven minute chit-chat about who's right and wrong and you don't want to get this matter settled. Supermarkets are not the place to get matters settled. You want to save time and get outside where the good stuff is going on.

You'll find more "which-is-the-fastest-line" clues as you get into the rhythm of one-person household supermarket shopping. You won't have an exasperated or frantic look on your face because grocery shopping is not one of those things that stirs your soul. Fabulous restaurants stir your soul. In the supermarket, you're content and calm as you read tabloids and juicy newspapers as you're going through the speedy line.

There is only one exception to all the above: when you're going to be serving delicacies to people at your house. This is called pleasure shopping and this is a wonderful time to shilly-shally over your ingredients in anticipation of your wonderful brunch, lunch, dinner, barbecue, or midnight snack to be held at your semi-clean house.

Although a lot of details are given here about cutting time at the supermarket, every minute you spend on this subject is worth it to your fantastic single-householder life.

So enough on the three main household duties — cleaning, laundry, and shopping. I can't go into the other household chores, like cleaning closets and rearranging bathroom cabinets, it's just too much to think about. Do the best you can. I'm exhausted just thinking of the three main things.

There's no doubt about it. A person living alone should try to get enough money to have someone take care of all these things.

5

Emergencies.
Try Not to
Have Any

Another way to keep your one-person household running smoothly is to keep emergencies to a minimum.

This may sound glib. You might be saying to yourself, "Well, either they happen or they don't." True. But we can use a little forethought in preventing some disasters.

Here are a few of the rock-solid reasons for keeping emergencies to a minimum during the time we're living as one-person householders:

1. No one's right there to help.
2. An emergency drains energy. (We must use all our concentration to keep calm when all we want to do is yell, cry, and gnash our teeth — which would offer us some form of relief. But no, we have to stay calm and figure out a way to get out of the emergency.)
3. Emergencies are very time-consuming. They prevent us from doing the great things we had planned to do.
4. Emergencies are depressing. We usually sit in the middle of our one-person emergency and say, with a pathetic look on the face as we pound our fist on the table, "Why me! Why me!"
5. There's no one around to feel sorry for us during the emergency. Help usually comes after the emergency is over.
6. An emergency upsets one's equilibrium and makes a person cranky.

Here are some ways we can reduce emergencies.

1. We should think before we stand on a rickety chair to reach *anything* at the top of a closet.
2. We should think before we pick up a heavy piece of furniture.

(We should face the furniture straight on, not sideways, and lift with our legs, not our backs. How many times have we heard this.)

3. We should think before we buy rugs that don't have rubber backings. They slip, and we slip with them.

4. We should think before we wash our windows, sitting on the sill, leaning backwards. (Let a professional person wash your windows backwards.)

5. We should think before we wash kitchen knives when we're in an angry mood. A knife knows when we're angry, and it helps us by nicking us to make us even angrier. This goes for anything sharp: a razor, a lawnmower, a scissor.

6. Look into personal emergency response systems that will come to the house at the tap of an electronic unit. These guys can save the day and might be just what you need for peace of mind. For a small monthly charge they're available to you whenever an emergency strikes. All you have to do is push a button. The services are called medical alert systems or lifeline systems. Your local health agency may be able to answer questions and help you locate a program in your area.

One thing I'll never do again is to move heavy furniture after a breakup of a romance. I remember the evening so well.

The romance had broken up during the day, and as evening came about I put on moody records and sulked. Then I glared at the furniture in my living room and said, "Something's got to change here!" I lugged bookcases across the room. I moved the sofa from one wall to another. Then, the ultimate, I tried to lift a cabinet filled with LP (not compact) records, as well as heavy encyclopedias — about 200 pounds. The cabinet smashed down on my index finger, right hand. The finger bled like crazy.

I was so morose I didn't care about the accident. Everything seemed futile. I finally, in the most dejected way, wrapped gauze around the finger and bandaged it. At least I had my wits about me to do that. But to this day, I have the scar on the top of my right index finger reminding me of an emergency of a one-person householder. If someone had been there, no doubt we would have had the sense to get the cut stitched up or do something to make the finger look proper again.

When I see the scar on that prominent first finger, I say to myself, "Would you please not move furniture when you're in an emotional state?" I usually answer, "Yes."

You'll want to think first before doing superhuman things around your household — or else you'll be fraught with pulled muscles, cuts, nicks, and assorted disasters you don't have time for.

This doesn't mean that as people living alone we have to become scared rabbits and never do anything around the place — but it means not to make maniacs out of ourselves either.

It's simply smart not to do major or dangerous household jobs without another person there. It's just like the old swimming motto: take a buddy with you when you're swimming in deep water.

Although the finger-mutilation problem was gruesome, the one incident that really put the whole subject of emergencies into perspective for me was the day I picked up a fragile antique desk.

I simply wanted to move the desk from one room in my apartment to another. I had lifted it and moved it many times before; it weighed about fifteen pounds (contents included).

This day, however, I didn't think before I acted. I turned towards the desk at an angle — I wasn't facing it squarely and I didn't stand in front of it properly. Not only was I at an awkward angle, I tried to lift it with my back, not my legs.

It took only three seconds for something to snap in my back. I gasped with excruciating pain and flipped backwards on the living room carpet. So there I was, looking up at the ceiling saying, "Now what."

If I tried moving an inch to the right, to the left, or up or down, I felt I would scream with pain. However, no neighbor was close enough to hear a scream, so I didn't bother with that.

I thought, "I'm going to die on my living room carpet. I can't move an inch and I can't even get to the phone. Even if the phone rings, I can't get up to answer it."

I was on my back, immobilized by the pain, for over an hour. I certainly memorized my ceiling's paint job in that time. All I could do was stare straight up.

During that hour I envisioned myself turning into a skeleton in three days if nobody came by and found me in my plight. I thought cobwebs would grow from my body to the wall, as in the cartoons. I thought, Whatta way to die. Because of moving a desk.

It became clear to me that an emergency is a drawback to someone in a one-person household. THERE IS NO HELP. *We* have to figure out what to do.

I finally became methodical in my thinking. I remembered movies where someone with a broken *anything* used movement — slight at first, then a bit more, then more, to the injured area.

For the next two hours, I wiggled a finger, I wiggled a toe, I wiggled my ears. I tried to lift my back a quarter of an inch off the floor. I tried to tell the body it had to do something, or else we'd be in this position for days and we'd get hungry.

I finally got up in a bent-over position and walked hunchback to a chair. Then I slowly got up again and made my way to a chair by the phone. Ah. Now we're getting somewhere, I thought. I called a friend and told her that I couldn't move and what did she recommend.

She brought over a "heat with moisture" heating pad, just what I needed. I used it for a few hours, and now could stand up at least semi-straight. I could even go to work the next day, although I was a very slumped-over and strange-looking employee. I was fairly miserable.

But it taught me something. I now put some thinking in before I do major household moves. Should I lift it? Or should I hire a pro-fessional to come in and do the job or ask a friend to come over and help.

Just because we live alone doesn't mean we have to be so self-sufficient that we can't ask for help.

People like to help when they're really needed, especially if they know you're not going to ask them for *everything* you need done.

Once I had a wisdom tooth pulled, and the pulling left me with a fever and incapacitated for a week. I wasn't able to hobble in and out of my apartment to get what I needed and my larder wasn't stocked.

A friend of mine — without even asking if I needed groceries and other things — simply showed up with two bags of wonderful food. She picked out things she ordinarily ate, and I had food in my cupboards I'd never seen before — herbed cream cheese; canned lobster bisque; peppercorn pate; and snacking crackers from Holland. I ate those things with such appreciation, not only for the food value, but for the friend value.

Once I had been out sick and hadn't gone in to work for three days. On the fourth day, I said to myself, "Oh, well, they'll know I'm sick and won't worry about me, so I won't phone." Soon after, my phone rang and I gurgled a "hello."

The head of my department said that everyone had been worried the past hour when I hadn't called. They thought that since I was living alone, anything could have happened and they wanted to know if I was OK.

The people in my department mostly live in the suburbs and have families, and hadn't experienced the live-by-yourself life. They were concerned about someone living alone, and they checked in to see if everything was OK. I was touched.

The next day, my department head shrugged the whole thing off (when I thanked him and the group for calling) by saying: "Well, we all had visions of flies hovering around your lifeless body in your living-alone state, and that's why we called." But it was a caring thing that had been done.

People do care for those of us in a one-person household. But we should try to have as few emergencies as possible. They ain't fun.

So keep things running smoothly, keep emergencies to a minimum, keep a smile on your face, and, by all means, don't go up and fix the roof of your house by yourself.

6 Don't Stay Alone Too Long, You'll Turn Funny

There are occasions when you haven't invited anyone over, and no one has invited you anywhere. These stretches of nothing-going-on can happen for no reason and can come completely out of the blue, and you'll say: "Why is Nothing Going On?"

Then a little bit of paranoia seeps in, and you'll say, "Maybe it's me. Maybe I'm a creep and no fun." You'll busy yourself around the house, have injured feelings, and you'll think, "Well, I don't care. I don't need anyone." You're ticked off at the world.

You heave a big sigh and say grumpily to yourself, *"Fine!* It's a great time to do all the household/lawn/car/garage chores that are piled up waiting for me." You make a list of your chores, look at them, put the list on a table, and go take a nap. There's no rush in getting the chores done. You've got nothing to do for the next few days except chores, so you don't have to hurry and get them done all at once.

When you get up, you're still pondering why your social life has degenerated to nothing and why you don't have *any* activities lined up. Things had been going pretty well lately, enough things to do, enough people to see. Now this nothingness.

Not only has no one made plans with you, which hasn't done your ego any good, you haven't extended yourself to people, either. Why bother with people who haven't cared enough to call to say they want to see you?

You can see you've got a situation on your hands, that can snowball, that has all the ingredients for strangeness.

And this goes on for two and a half days.

Now you've turned funny.

Here are some of the ways you'll know that you've turned funny — and some solutions to the problem.

41

Circumstance #1: You mentally re-hash a PROBLEM YOU'RE HAVING WITH A FRIEND. You go over it in your mind for the 800th time. "It's his/her fault! Why didn't he/she call me?! Why do I have to be the one to call? It's not my fault! Why did he/she start this problem!" Then the tape starts all over again, for the *801st* time: It's his/her fault! Why didn't he/she call... and so on. The hot motor in your brain won't stop whirring. It's caught in a Catch 22. It doesn't want to think about the situation, but it can't stop — because there's nothing and no one around to break off the escalation of heated thinking.

Solution #1: Call a neighbor and a friend across town and listen to *their* problems. Then order in Chinese dinner and watch *anything* on TV.

Sometimes, however, trying to perk yourself up doesn't work, and then what you should do is *just plain sulk.* Sulk, sulk, sulk. You get so tired of sulking and feeling sorry about your problem and everything in the world in general, and all of a sudden a ray of sunlight hits your emotions and you're OK. A good sulk is sometimes better than spending hours and days of brain power over the situation.

Circumstance #2: When you start STARING at your hands, or anything else, for more than fifteen minutes, you've turned funny.

Solution #2: Go out and buy *People* magazine and *The Star* tabloid newspaper, buy a pizza or fried chicken, come home and figure out how to get famous, or rich, or happy, or all three.

Circumstance #3: When your MONEY problems are constantly tumbling around in your head — before you go to sleep; when you wake; throughout the time you eat breakfast, lunch, and dinner — you've turned funny. You think your whole life is a flop because you don't have enough money coming in to pay Visa and a lot of other folks.

Solution #3: Find a friend (*not* an accountant or a financial expert who's going to lecture you); with that friend, *discuss* your money problems, bring them out in the open and let them get some air. Talk to your friend about how awful it feels to have these difficulties nipping at your heels. A lack of money is not quite enough to drive us stark, raving mad, it's just enough to make us jittery and irritable all day long.

In all likelihood, the friend with whom you've chosen to break your code of secrecy will tell you horror stories of his or her own. You'll both end up laughing, the "laughter" chemical we mentioned before will squirt throughout your body, and you're back on the track of being a *non* semi-crazed person (as you were when you kept re-hashing this money business only to yourself). It's amazing what the company of one human being can do to lessen the mental turmoil of another human being.

Circumstance #4: Another thing that will make you turn funny is mulling over PAST RELATIVE PROBLEMS. You mull, mull, and then mull some more about why your little brother Sammy hit you over the head when you were seven years old. Not only did he hit, he hid your favorite sweater. You couldn't find the sweater for weeks, until your mother said you had to sweep and mop the floor of your room. With absolute disbelief, as you were brooming things out from under your bed, there was your sweater in a corner among all the dustballs. How could he stoop so low.

Solution #4: Sammy had problems of his own. He had the same set of parents as you did, and he wasn't the perfect kid. A lot of people in the world aren't perfect. Even if Sammy is still a brat now, thirty years later, forget it. You can't change a person, but you can step to one side and stay out of his way when he comes at you like a buzz-saw. Turn off this relative problem. Instead, sign up for a course in "Body Massage for Couples." Call up a friend to be the other body in the couple. When you're getting a massage, you definitely aren't thinking about relatives.

Circumstance #5: The Granddaddy of ways to turn funny is to TURN NUMB by not having any interaction with anyone — by phone or in person — for a prolonged period of time.

You get a gray and glazed feeling around every part of you: your eyes, your thinking process, your ambition, your energy, and your interest in *anything* — friend problems, money problems, staring problems, or relative problems — they all go down the drain when you're in this state. Your body has sensed no other human contact for a certain amount of time, and it has shifted into another zone of existence. Your emotions have been numbed with mental novocaine.

During this period, what you'll enjoy doing most is wearing your tattered and spotted bathrobe over your wrinkled pajamas. You'll eat out of cans, and this is the *one* time you're allowed to eat over the sink. There will be dishes piled up all around the kitchen, but you won't care. You'll read the newspaper once, twice, and three times a day to see if you missed anything. You'll occasionally feel a rush of worry about things to be repaired or cleaned in your house, but this will soon go away. You're too numb to think about such things. You'll go take a nap in your bed, under the covers, with your robe and slippers on. You'll watch daytime TV, nighttime TV, 2:00, 3:00, and 4:00 A.M. TV.

When the phone rings, you won't answer it. You'll say, "Go away. If I don't pick up the phone they'll think I'm out. So there."

You've gone to the dumps, totally.

Solution #5: There is only one answer to the above. I've found that it works every time. Go out and be with a person.

This is where a nine-to-five job comes in handy. At least every Monday morning you know you'll be with people again, whether you want to or not.

If you don't have a job that you have to report to the next day, then do this: bathe, go to bed at a reasonable time of night, set your clock to get up and go SOMEPLACE the next day — to a class, to a place where you're needed, to a department store, to a bookstore to find a self-help book about What to Do When the Blahs Hit. There's nothing like getting a little spiffed up and going out of the house doing things, and *talking.* You're back in the human race. (There have been times, when I haven't talked to someone in two days, my voice got so high and croaky I could hardly be heard when I talked to someone again. My vocal chords had atrophied.)

After getting yourself out in the world, you'll find you're ready to talk at length to a person. So you arrange to see him or her. You don't have to *do* anything with the person, except talk. Although doing something, even dinner, adds some spice to the get-together.

By the way, getting out of the house and going to a museum or a movie by yourself will not stop you from being numb. It might be a surface solution, but it's not a long-lived one, because you still haven't talked to anyone except the ticket seller to say, "One ticket, please."

You'll find other circumstances and solutions cropping up at odd moments when you've fallen in the trap of being alone too long.

There are times, however, when it might be OK to wallow in a circumstance that has turned you funny. It might be Mother Nature's way of having you stop the world and get off for a while.

The important thing is not to stay funny too long. That's all you have to remember about this subject.

The Weekdays. Including
7   the Phenomenon
of Monday Morning

Well, here you are with your Time Chart stretched out in front of you (see page 28). It's Sunday night and a whole week is ahead of you. Hopefully the Time Chart has sections blocked out by invitations you've received and other sashays out of the house, as well as notations of chunks of time you've put aside for projects you're working on. You are, after all, an on-the-go and no-grass-growing-under-your-feet person.

Weekdays were invented mainly to Get Things Done. Even if you don't want to Get Things Done, the activity buzzing around you nags at you and makes you feel guilty if you're not participating.

One weekday morning, I simply didn't want to get up and go to work. I said, "I've had it, I give that company my conscientious best when I'm there, I deserve at least one weekday off for my mental health." I was going to stay in my comfortable bed and sleep luxuriously late.

Then my clock radio came on with the news: a transit strike had occurred in New York, and there were no trains, buses, or subways for commuters. I thought, "Well, there you are. What a great excuse for staying home. Probably no one's going to work today."

Then the newscast said that commuters in New Jersey, Connecticut, and Long Island were surging through the heaviest traffic of the century to get to work. Over and over I heard about how valiant they were, how nothing was going to stop them from getting to work in the city. People were even walking miles across the Brooklyn Bridge and the 59th Street Bridge from the outer boroughs.

After the pluck and grit and determination of the commuters had been described for the fiftieth time, I caved in.

It was the Long Island people on the Long Island Expressway that did it for me. According to the radio weather report, in addition to the mess on the roads, it was a bleak, dreary, and drizzly morning, too. (I still hadn't gotten out of bed to look out a window.)

In my mind's eye, seeing those hunched-over drivers inching along at two miles an hour on the gray, wet LIE, surrounded by monstrous tractor-trailer trucks, was too much for me. I thought: if half a million Long Islanders can struggle into Manhattan like salmon thrashing upriver, the least I could do was to get out of bed and walk the few blocks to my office.

That's the way the activity of other people on a weekday can work on us.

Now, about Monday mornings. Frankly, there are many people who have told me they simply don't have that "up and at 'em" feeling during this particular time of the work week. Who wants to be "Up." Who wants to be "At 'Em." The bed feels so warm and comfortable and the realities of the world seem so far away.

Psychologists have a long explanation for it, but to put it briefly, they say that not liking Monday mornings is a pretty common human reaction. And by noon on Monday, if you've gotten out of bed, the creakiness, crankiness, and haziness will disappear and you'll feel comfortable out in the world again.

One of the best feelings to come out of any weekday is the feeling of accomplishment at the end of the day: you've persevered, you've completed Project X, and you're proud of yourself. Project X can range from planting roses to finishing off a million-dollar deal. You'll want your week filled up with as many Project X's as you can handle — all stemming from your needs, your interests, and even your job.

So you have the feeling of accomplishment at the end of the day. Now you should either: 1) Plop and do nothing or 2) Do something fantastic. We all know how to do each of these things. You have your own way of plopping when you come home, and you have your own favorite choices of something fantastic to do.

As a person living alone, don't forget that you get to pick what you want to do on weekdays, when you want to do it, with whom, and exactly how to do it. No one is saying to you, First I want you to pick this up, drive there, go here, and I want you to clean this up and mow the lawn, and on and on and on.

You're the engineer of your weekday happenings.

*"Oh, everything's about the same here
at the office—the usual trendy simmering admixture
of ambition, greed, betrayal and sex."*

Weekdays are the workhorses of life. Don't let them slip away from you just because you're living alone and there's no one there to spur you on. Keep a journal of what you do on weekdays.

I won't talk about the bummer parts of weekdays — the dentist, the appointment with the IRS, the car repair shop, the Motor Vehicles Bureau, and the crowded bus. No sense feeling sorry for ourselves because we have to visit these territories once in a while. Everybody does.

Squeeze everything you can out of weekdays. They're given to us for a reason.

(Except for Monday mornings. I find no reason for them. Especially for them to start so early. I wish Monday mornings would start at noon.)

8

The Weekends. The Good, the Bad, and the Exquisite

Now we're onto something. For a person living alone, a weekend can be sensational or a disaster for reasons that only affect our living-alone lifestyle.

The kind of weekends I like are sensational ones.

In this case, everything goes right. We come out of the weekend feeling adored, exhausted from late-night good times, and maybe a little achy from doing some sporty thing. We feel life's great, our friends and relatives are great, and we're great. We've been fulfilled by mental, physical, and rib-tickling activities with people who suit us just right.

I hit on one of these weekends about six times a year. A person living alone knows exactly how satisfying they are. They are to be savored. Here are some of my favorites:

● Go to the Bahamas just for the weekend.

● Go up to New England or Florida or to the country in New Jersey to visit my favorite cousins.

● Tackle a big household project, like wallpaper or painting, and order in food every night and eat it with a friend.

● Be with my dancing friends at night and with my tennis friends during the day.

● Go to a vacation hideaway at the seashore with a favorite chum.

We can all think of luscious weekends pertinent to us.

The other side of the coin, however, is the weekend that is so far down in the pits that you're seeing the "underbellies of snakes." (You can't get much lower than this.)

It all starts on Thursday. You realize that you don't have any plans for the weekend, and you say, "Well, that's OK, something will turn up, I'm not going to panic, and maybe I need a do-nothing

49

weekend." So Friday night, after a week of accomplishments and being busy doing things that must be done, you're glad to have nothing to do.

You really don't *want* anything to do at this point, and you're happy you can read the paper for an hour, fix a meal that's out of the ordinary, watch a nighttime soap opera, watch the late movie, and go to bed late. But then Saturday arrives, and the phone still hasn't rung. You say, "Fine. Just what I wanted. Peace and quiet."

Inside, I know it's really not what I want — and nothing seems to go on all weekend long. Alone is OK, but enough is enough. Saturday night comes and goes, Sunday arrives, and you seem to be stuck in a time warp. It's just an odd circumstance that absolutely nothing is going on with you and other people.

After a weekend like this, Monday morning can look pretty good. At least banks and post offices and all sorts of offices are open again, and you can get on your busy workhorse and have dealings with people.

When Monday morning comes, people might ask you, "How was your weekend?" Simply say, (now this is important): "IT WAS GREAT." Then talk about other things.

I'm not saying that barren social weekends happen only to people who live alone. I've talked to a lot of people who live all sorts of ways who say they really had a rotten weekend.

So hang in there, the following weekend you could be flying off to Rio.

But we, as people living by ourselves, have got to be sure our attitudes haven't become negative, or that we've gotten into a rut and are simply not doing things or seeing enough people. If this is the case, we've got to take ourselves by the shoulders and shake ourselves into taking action to remedy the weekends.

The third type of weekend is simply the middle-of-the-road type; we do a little bit of this, a little bit of that. For the most part, a good medium weekend means no catastrophes, you're at peace with the world, you're fairly happy with yourself, and you can manage to give yourself a pat on the back for keeping your life together in a snazzy sort of way.

Now, after experiencing:
1. The Sensational Weekend
2. The Pits Weekend
3. The Medium Weekend

I've found that the *ultimate* weekend for me is to work on a project

I'm so interested in that the two days go by like five minutes.

You know what these weekends are like. You might have been starting a new business venture, or were taking part in a political campaign just before election time: you were deeply and happily immersed in something you felt strongly about.

You've seen the movies where the scientist is in the lab and can't even take time to eat a sandwich; the musician practices and practices until his hands get stiff; the author types away surrounded by reams of paper oblivious to everything; the physicist draws numbers and formulas all over the blackboard with a deliriously blissful expression on his or her face.

When your project absorbs you this way on a weekend (or whenever you have open-ended time), all time and space leave you and you're in a state of euphoria.

In a way, you've removed yourself from the world, but you're more part of the world than ever before. You're involved. You're not a spectator. For this weekend, you're a participant and you're adding something to the world.

When all your decks get clear enough to get to the point of pouring something back *into* civilization, you'll have had the very best weekend of all.

Your Food Habits. Why Are They Different From Everyone Else's?

9

This is what happens with the person living alone and food: there is no one right by your elbow or knee when you shop for it, store it, cook it, eat it, or clean up after eating it. It ends up being a very cut-and-dried activity, which in the long run is to your benefit. You'll soon see why.

Naturally, the system I'm going to promulgate may not apply to all one-person householders. Some people may want to spend lots and lots of hours shopping for and cooking gourmet meals for themselves every day. I prefer to save these types of meals for when I'm having company over, giving a party, going to a party, or eating at you-know-where, fabulous restaurants.

Many people, when they first live alone, keep the house stocked as if a whole family lived there. There's a big bag of potatoes under the sink, a gallon of ice cream in the freezer, an extra-large loaf of bread, a basket of apples, a five-pound bag of flour, and ten pounds of pork chops bought on sale. After a few weeks, they'll see that the food never goes away! They chip away and chip away at it when they eat their meals, but unless they have a sit-down dinner for twenty people these large amounts of food constantly stare out at them when they open the cupboards and refrigerator. And what's to be done about it? Have you ever eaten apples and pork chops for weeks in a row?

Also, making big pots of anything for yourself (spaghetti, stew, chili, chicken gumbo) will create roadblocks for you. First you say to yourself, "I'll solve this stupid cooking problem. I'll cook just once a week, on Sunday, and then eat it all week." Let me tell you, you'll never see "the picture of the rabbit" on the bottom of the pot, because you'll never see the bottom of the pot! On Day Four of eat-

ing "Hot-Pot-Food-X," you won't want to ever see it or eat it again.

Then you say, "OK, I'll take what's left and put aluminum foil around it and make a nice little package and put it in the freezer." When this happens often enough, you'll open your freezer door one day and recoil from the angry glare of all those foil packets piled one on another. And you'll say, "Who wants to thaw out left-overs and eat them. Phew!" Besides this, there will be no room for your precious ice cubes in the aluminum-stuffed freezer — ice cubes that you use to serve guests delectable and charming drinks as you loll about having fun and witty conversations solving your (and the world's) problems.

Soon you'll find that "streamlining" is the answer. Get the BASIC food you need every week (with occasional luxuries thrown in so you don't feel like you've been sent to prison). Basic foods are simple fare, but in time and calories saved, they're worth getting each week — and only in the quantities you can consume in one week. Here they are: meat, fish, poultry, potatoes or other starch, fruit, leafy greens and other salad makings, milk, eggs, bread. We all know that list by heart.

Other than those items that are staples (salt, pepper, coffee), as well as one or two of your favorite items (peanut butter, Sara Lee Cheesecake), the above basics should be the only things to have at your beck and call. Cook them simply in few pots and you've got it made. You've saved shopping time, preparation time, calories, and clean-up time, and you're eating healthy (miracle of miracles) foods.

When Thoreau was asked what the most important piece of philosophical advice he could give the world would be, he shouted, "Simplify! Simplify! Simplify!"

And why especially do we want to simplify in the food area? Because we don't want lots of those white spaces in the Time Chart filled in with words like "Cooking," "Grocery Shopping," "Doing Dishes and Cleaning Up in Kitchen." We want things like: "Planning Trip to Bangkok," "Dancing at the Rainbow Room," or "Meeting Joe at Restaurant Luxurioso."

Now having wonderful basic foods in your house most of the time doesn't mean your house shouldn't smell and have the sound of food. One man I know says the minute he comes in from a workday he puts a pot of water on to boil, then puts brown rice in to cook, and he hears it bubbling and it gives him a feeling "something is going on." I throw a small potato in the oven most nights — while I'm working, reading, stewing, or mulling things over. It makes me feel "something is going on," and it gives me a familiar and cuddly aroma that I remember from childhood.

So eating simple fare doesn't mean you cut off all sensations of scent, taste, and sound of food. It's still there.

A beginner live-aloner can fall into traps of crazy eating. Crazy eating over a long period of time does not benefit anyone, except the manufacturer of Pringles potato chips.

One of the traps is thinking: "Oh boy! I can eat whatever I want," and then trotting out to the grocery store and loading up with donuts, cake, frozen pizza, soft drinks, salami, bologna, and everything else that is, as we all know, the most delicious food in the entire world.

After a few weeks of these items, however, your energy starts to wane, your skin gets sallow looking, your hair looks like a shoe brush, and you've gained fifteen pounds. We have to remember that most things we bring into the house will end up inside of *us*, and if we simply don't bring them home, the problem is solved. Fortunately, with this "goodies-all-over-the-house" game plan, it's live and learn — and back to the drawing board of finding the right foods.

Another trap is to eat "Just Anything" — having a bowl of some kind of glop for dinner, washing the bowl, and tossing the bowl back into the cupboard. This is awful. You're telling yourself that you're not even worth fixing a meal for, and who needs to be told that? Will you be an amazing, confident, and classy person with a message like that lodged in your psyche?

Granted, we all do the "just-make-it-a-fast-glop-bowl" routine once in a while, but having it most nights of the week is not an up thing to do for dinner.

Some people say, "Oh, to heck with it. I'll just eat at the local coffee shop every night." Nothing wrong with this, but you could also be at home with your baked-potato smell in the house, dancing the new steps you learned, and listening to your favorite Rudy Vallee, Frank Sinatra, or Bruce Springsteen records while answering the phone and talking to all those people who think you're so charming they want to invite you to their place for dinner the next night. (OK, this might be a tad puffed up, but being at home making things happen has to be better than sitting at the counter of a coffee shop staring at the lemon meringue pie and single-serving boxes of

Wheaties and Extra-K Cornflakes.)

By the way, doing the basic food-cooking stuff in your house in the evening will, on an average, take no more than thirty minutes: take it out of the refrigerator, wash it, chop anything if necessary, put it in pots and cook it.

One final trap is to use food as "entertainment" throughout the day and evening. There's no getting around it, people living alone or even people living with a lot of other people get BORED with the daily A's to Z's of life. Most of us are wondering why we aren't Donald Trump with eight limousines and two helicopters taking us wherever we want to go. Life's unfair. Why do I have to wait for buses? Let's eat-eat-eat something; it's so quick, easy, reliable, and entertaining to our teeth, tongue, and tastebuds.

I used to wonder, when I was growing up, why people said they were "entertaining" when all they were doing was inviting people over for dinner. I thought, "Where's the entertainment? Are there going to be clowns? Or a band? Why do they call it 'entertaining' when all they're going to do is serve dinner on a table with maybe drinks before in the living room?"

Well, now I know. Most people consider eating an entertainment, which it certainly can be.

But when you've got long stretches of time in front of you and you use food to feel entertained, something's out of whack. Believe me, I've been out of whack many times, that's why I know so much about it. But when I'm not using food as constant entertainment, then things are going right.

For example, I'm so interested in writing this book that eating a small carton of cottage cheese puts something in my stomach, makes me feel like I've been fed, and I don't want to think about eating a lot of super-duper foods. I'm interested in another activity, and food rates low on my interest scale now.

But I'll eat my fuddy-duddy nutritious dinner later on, just as a habit like brushing my teeth, and that will be that with "another evening of food."

Food traps are always waiting, but if you experience them and beat them at their game, things will look up.

You'll also want to have other meals, besides dinner, that contain basic food. Eggs or cereal for breakfast, for instance, no fancy pancakes and imported Maine syrup. You don't want to spend time whipping and dipping batters for a precious hour. Eat your egg and forget it and get on to other activities.

Don't make your lunch a horrible concoction of leftovers out of the refrigerator. There's *nothing* more depressing than gluey gray-brown food for lunch. Anyway, if you eat your Basic Simple Fare meal in the evening, you won't have any leftovers: you cooked and ate your portion of chicken/fish/meat, your potato, your vegetable, and that was that. Over and done with, no tidbits left on little plates.

Make yourself something decent and quick for lunch. You'll get the hang of what's "decent and quick" as time goes on. It will be food that doesn't make you feel like an orphan.

As you eat your tidy, nutritious dinners some nights, your mind might stray to thoughts about big family meals. You might do into work the next day and hear about wonderful meals people had with one's wife/husband and 2.3 kids: nine courses of everything from Italian appetizers, to Swedish meatballs, to the main course of lobster, with many side dishes, to a selection of four desserts. And this is just a weekday meal.

This is what comes into my ears as I sit in my office and overhear the talk in the hallways from the men who are married. They seem to enjoy telling each other what was served the night before. And if there is a little "can you top this?" involved, who cares.

This brings up a good topic.

A while ago there was an article written called "Everyone Needs a Wife."

The article upset some people, confused others, and illuminated the mindsets of others.

The simple point was: We ALL would like to have someone around taking care of our basics: laundry, food, housekeeping.

The person who wrote the article used "wife" as a generic term meaning "caretaker."

There's an example from George Burns. He writes about the wonderful couple who live at his place and take care of all his domestic duties, including fixing all his meals. See? This is great (if affordable).

However, if one doesn't have a "wife/couple/caretaker" around and we are 100% live-aloners, what does one do?

The best we can. Which, in the case of our "daily bread," means treating ourselves decently with tasty, nutritious food that doesn't take an afternoon to prepare.

This is an area to be reckoned with, because the minute your eating habits to down the drain, so does your psyche.

I'm not saying we have to be Pollyannaish about eating well. Sometimes I get fed up with feeding myself properly. So for a few days I go off the wagon and eat cottage cheese from cartons; slices of cheese straight out of the packet with no intention of making it into a sandwich; handfuls of unadorned lettuce taken straight off the (washed!) head; tomatoes eaten like apples from the hand; cucumber slices with the skins still on and eaten right there and then; and good old Cup-A-Soup that only requires boiling water.

During these few days, there are no such hours called "mealtime" at my house. I don't know the difference between breakfast, lunch, or dinner. They're all the same: odd.

After two or three days of this, I don't feel good about it. My life is going downhill. At that point, I probably will call a friend and go out and have a good old-fashioned real meal at a comfortable restaurant. Then I put my life back on the track, with real breakfasts, lunches, and dinners.

I suppose everyone who fixes food day in and day out falls by the wayside every once in a while. Routines encourage revolt. There's no getting around it.

Now. One of my favorite ways of acquiring food is from airlines. One of the reasons I like to clamber onto a plane, other than to travel, is to have airline food and drinks. I know every standup comic has jokes about how awful airline food is, but I, for one, am a fan of airline food. (It seems especially good if I'm getting it after one of my odd hodgepodge eating periods at home.)

There's such an element of *surprise* when you eat on an airplane. You don't have to plan it, shop for it, cook it, or serve it. You have no say in the matter of what you're going to get. We're talking total surprise.

It starts out with the suspense of what kind of nuts you're going to get with your drink before the meal. Honey roasted peanuts? Smoked almonds? Cashews? Will the person sitting next to me be eating his or her salted nuts? Can I have them if they don't want them? Would the attendant give me two bags if I asked for them? (They don't seem to encourage this. I think they only have one bag per passenger, and that's it.)

Now, the next thing: where is the food cart going to start? At the top of the aisle where I'm sitting? Or all the way in the back, which means I have to wait a half hour to get my tray of wonderful things.

The suspense is killing me.

All of a sudden the attendants come rushing through the curtains from first class pushing a stainless steel cart. They stop at the top of the aisle right by my row. I've won.

I overhear the choices they're giving the people across the aisle. My mouth waters, and visions of food, food, food (prepared and served by someone else!) swirl through my brain. The event is making me heady.

They're saying, "Do you want Barbequed Beef Ribs or Lasagna?" Or: Do you want Roast Chicken or Salisbury Steak?" "Turkey with Stuffing or Beef Stew?"

And these are complete meals...no hit or miss affairs.

I get my tray put in front of me, let's say Barbequed Beef Ribs. My eyes dance.

When do I ever cook Barbequed Beef Ribs for myself at home? Never. But the airline has cooked it for me.

Not only that, there's so much other stuff on the tray with it: green beans and some kind of seasoned rice are crowded together on the Entree segment of my compartmentalized tray along with the gloriously glazed Barbequed Beef Ribs.

And what do we have here? A little plastic container of creamy Italian dressing. When do I ever serve myself creamy Italian dressing at home? It's minimal no-nonsense oil and vinegar at home.

And look at that salad. With strips of red cabbage, chunks of grapefruit, Bibb lettuce, slivered almonds. I mean, that's a salad.

Then I've also got silverware, salt, pepper, and butter in packets. Packets, packets everywhere, filled with everything the Food and I need.

And look at that beautiful hard roll. Harder-crusted rolls I have never found as I find on airlines. I don't know how they get them so hard; it keeps passengers busy trying to break them.

One airline I travel on a lot served something called English Soda Bread Made With Malt. How's that for exotic?

As I happily chomp on my meal and chat with my seat-mate, I'm in heaven. And the dessert still awaits. What surprise dessert do we have today? It could be a one and one-half inch pineapple cheesecake; three chocolate-covered pretzels; two macaroons in fluted paper cup; a tiny square of chocolate cake with fudge icing; a cherry tart; vanilla pudding with coconut.

How can anyone say they don't enjoy airline food. The tray is loaded with surprises and good things from corner to corner.

I'm talking mainly about lunches and dinners on airlines, because at breakfast time they seem to just plunk anything down in front of you — no discussions and not very many surprises. They seem to be very big on scrambled eggs at the airlines. Since I rarely fly early in the morning, I don't get too many of their scrambled eggs. But lunches and dinners are another matter.

When I go out to the West Coast to visit my mother, I take a super-saver flight that has me changing planes in Chicago, so I get two full meals in five hours: Lunch on the way to Chicago, and a big luscious dinner while flying over the Rockies. When I get to my mother's house, she has another meal fixed for me. All in all, I've had quite a day of good food service.

My mother and I have English Soda Bread Made With Malt with our meal. It comes in dainty little cellophane packets stamped with an American Airlines logo. Later on we nibble on morsels of chocolate covered pretzels, again with the American Airlines logo.

What heaven an airline flight is. I can't think of anything better than a window seat, a pleasant seat-mate, a good book, and all those surprises awaiting in the galley for my pleasure.

Now back to our one-person households again.

There's also a fun side of food and the person living alone. We're probably the only category of people in the world who CAN EAT WHENEVER WE WANT TO. People living with other people usually have set eating hours, and things are done on a routine basis. You, however, can eat peanut butter and crackers in bed at four in the morning; you can eat pickled herring for breakfast at three in the afternoon (after sleeping late from being out until 3:00 a.m. the night before) and no one will look at you with disparagement.

We must now take into account where we're going to sit and what we're going to look at while we're having our speedy, wholesome, basic, nutritious, live-alone meals. This is a decision of paramount importance, because under no circumstances do you want to feel sorry for yourself eating alone. My position is: I thoroughly believe in reading the paper, a book, or watching television while eating.

This is exactly the opposite of what the eating experts say. They say: sit down at your wonderful polished dining room table, with a cloth napkin on your lap, a tall candle in front of you, your crystal plate on an exotic Picasso placemat, and do nothing else but chew. And chew each bite twenty-eight times and think about what you're chewing and close your eyes and experience the taste and texture and smell and appearance of every chew.

This is fine, but this would definitely spook most people living alone. I say, OK, get stimulated by the food you're eating, but get some visual or mental stimulation while you're eating it.

I have an apartment on the fourteenth floor of a Manhattan high-rise building, and I have a terrace with trees and shrubs and flowers. (In the spring and summer, they're at their greenest, most beautiful, and most aromatic and flowery.) On the terrace, I have a large white table that seats six people. Inside my apartment I have no dining room and no dining room table. So I invite people over for Company Dinners during five months of the year: June, July, August, September, and October. When November comes around, the Schappert Company Dinner Season is over, and it's back to the inside of the apartment where I have only two slender brass tables in the living room that I use to eat on. It works out great. One I use for my plate, the other for something to drink. And I plop them right in front of the television and watch "Moonlighting" while eating my nutritious delicious meat/vegetable/etc./etc. dinner without feeling a bit guilty.

Eating soup in my non-dining room table apartment is also easy. Soup is always in a mug and one drinks it. No fuss, no bother, no slurping off a spoon. Any noodles and other dregs left at the bottom of the cup can easily be scooped out in a jiffy and eaten. So the soup problem is licked forever in my house.

There's another side to this Spartan and creative existence of eating streamlined meals on non-tables and various other places while watching TV or reading the newspaper. It is called "Having Company Over For Dinner."

I'm sure most of the world doesn't have my situation of the summertime-only company dinners. I know most people have dining room tables. This is good. This means you can invite people over *twelve* months out of the year and cook dinners for them and have fascinating conversations with them. This is a real bonanza. Inviting people over for anything, dinner, brunch, lunch, and midnight trysts, has a lot going for it.

For one thing, you can now prepare and eat an exciting meal. It's also fun to look for actual ingredients in the supermarket instead of just running in and out with your weekly basics. And it's good to think about preparing something for others. It nurtures your soul and makes you feel like a warm human being. Then, the evening of your dinner with favorite friends, your mind gets to mull over your favorite topics, and you feel happy and content. Ah. The life of the person who lives alone!

Now we have a view of why our eating habits are different and more varied than other people's.

Of course, when we dine alone, there are a few rules we should follow:

RULE #1: DON'T EAT OVER THE SINK. Not even a can of sardines, which, as you know, has oil oozing out of it the minute you open it. When the sardine can is fully open, that oil is not only going to drip into the sink, it's also going to plop on the front of your favorite bathrobe or your crisp, freshly clean, white shirt. These items of clothing will smell like sardines for a long time. One item that may possibly be allowed to be eaten over the sink is fat tomato sandwiches that squirt. But there aren't too many other exceptions, because eating over the sink causes too much wear and tear on our self-esteem and our feeling of self-worth. (By the way, eating over the sink usually involves standing over it, but our cover person on this book tried a fancy approach.)

RULE #2: DON'T EAT OUT OF THE POT. A burnt lip takes weeks to heal.

RULE #3: DON'T SCOOP PEANUT BUTTER FROM THE JAR WITH YOUR FINGER. The reason for this is you'll have a hard time getting the peanut butter out from under your fingernails.

RULE #4: DON'T HOLD A BOOK ON YOUR LAP AND EAT AT THE SAME TIME — UNLESS YOU DON'T MIND DRIPS. Most people like to eat drippy things and read a book — but there are consequences to the book page. (I many times bypass this rule when reading a steamy paperback novel. Steamy novels were meant to be read with drippy sandwiches.

RULE #5: DON'T DRINK OUT OF THE MILK OR ORANGE JUICE CONTAINER. Now this is a toughie. It's really great to drink out of a container when you don't want to wash a glass. So I say: break this rule. Do it. And get new containers of milk and juice when company is coming over — just to be sanitary about the matter.

RULE #6: DO WHAT YOU'VE ALWAYS BEEN TOLD TO DO. EAT BREAKFAST. Your body feels vacant and neglected if you don't. You can keep the time to a minimum at breakfast if you want. I eat breakfast in 6-1/2 minutes, which includes scrambling an egg right in the frying pan.

RULE #7: DON'T EAT OUT OF A CAN. See #5 above.

RULE #8: STASH USED PLATES IN THE SINK, OUT OF SIGHT. It's O.K. to pile used plates, pots, and other eating items in the sink, no matter how high the stack goes. All you have to do is squirt a lot of dishwashing detergent on them, plug up the sink, put a stream of hot water over everything, and pretty soon you won't see the plates and pots, only suds. You can keep dishes like this for at least a day.

RULE #9: DON'T TOSS NUTS AND JELLY BEANS INTO THE AIR HOPING YOU'LL HIT YOUR MOUTH. They won't make it to your mouth, your floor will be a mess, and your pet will get bonked on the head with flying missiles.

RULE #10: DON'T DRIBBLE OR MAKE SLOSHING AND SLOPPING NOISES. Unless this is your family heritage, it's good not to get into this habit at home too much — you'll carry it into the outside world when you're dining with the upper crust.

Most cultures of the world are designed around families or groups eating together during certain parts of the day. So we want to learn something new — the feeding and care of that wonderful human being in your one-person household in a way that keeps his or her morale high. You're the sole nurturing and feeding agent to that person in your house, so you want to do a good job.

To wrap up the food topic, let's say it's definitely a learning experience to buy, cook, and eat for one. Food is there to give you energy to live the delightful life that awaits you. It's not an all-consuming problem or an entertainment feature in your daily home life. It's food. It just *is*.

10

Your Sleep.
Most Important.
You Are Allowed
to Languish

I think sleep is the best thing ever put on earth. And for us, sleeping *when* and *how* we want is one of the high points of living alone.

Sleeping, napping, and dozing are good ways to let your brain come to a gliding halt. For once, you don't have to *do* anything.

I'm sure lots of electro-magnetic things are going on in our brains, and all sorts of active things are happening in our blood cells and other places in our bodies, but we're blissfully in another world.

Sleep is so delectable and refreshing, I try to do it as much as possible.

There are different ways people sleep. Some get tired early at night and wake up early. These people are called Larks and they actually talk and bustle around at 5:30 in the morning. This is fine. They're doing what they want and getting up when they want.

Then there those who like the late night, and they go to bed late. These folks find it odd, and don't particularly like the fact, that most of the world wakes up before it's even *light* out. To them six o'clock in the morning is still the middle of the night. These people are called Owls.

Neither of these types is right or wrong. We're all doing what our bodies are telling us. Larks, of course, have an advantage, because they're always ready and prepared to go anywhere at 6:00 A.M. Owls are not too happy about having to be anywhere early in the morning, but they begrudgingly go where they're supposed to go.

You'll know who's a Lark and who's an Owl by the expressions on the faces of people in the street early in the morning. Are they smiling, animated, and laughing? Or just the opposite.

At night, you'll know who's a Lark, because they all seem to get slightly vacant looks on their faces, they don't want to talk about anything deep-down and interesting. They get a tiny bit nebbish-like, and their favorite phrase (as they're yawning) is: "Gosh. I'm fading. I'm really tired. I guess I'll go to bed." (And it's only 9:30, the start of the best time of the day for Owls.)

The best thing for Larks and Owls to do is get together at three o'clock in the afternoon when both are near a mental peak.

I've read that Thomas Edison and Albert Einstein and others of their ilk felt adequately refreshed on four hours sleep a night. Some of the world's corporate leaders have reduced this to three hours sleep a night, and then they bounce back to their boardrooms at 5:45 A.M. and have Power Breakfasts with the great and mighty.

I don't know what's escaping me here, but this doesn't connect with me. Just reading an article about Power Breakfasts makes me want to go to bed and pull the covers over my head. I know this is probably a wonderful level of existence, with lots of dollars coming in and power going out, but it's in the high stratosphere where the air is rarified.

Possibly we should all get to this point at some time. I believe it means we're super successful. If I ever get to the point of having Power Breakfasts, I'll write a book about it and share the secret delights of what goes on.

My favorite pastime is to SLEEP SLEEP SLEEP SLEEP SLEEP in a big cozy bed. Then, when I wake up, I'm a cheerful, charming person and not hostile to the world and to people around me.

Ever since I can remember, I've always been *woken up* when I truly felt like sleeping. I think I'm spending the rest of my life sleeping a lot to make up for being woken up.

Or maybe it started when I was put to bed when I was *wide awake*.

Something was being put out of order in my body's timeclock. The "Authorized Personnel" (my parents) were waking me up when I didn't want to wake up, and putting me to bed when I didn't want to go to sleep.

These tactics got to the point of being non-negotiable by the time I started kindergarten. "You've *got* to go to sleep at night so you can get up to go to school."

I was already frazzled.

I used to think that at 8:00 P.M. the best thing to do was flop down on the living room floor, read the comic strips in the newspaper, listen to a blaring radio, and pet the cat. The best part of the day.

Instead, I'm rushed around to a tub, washed, dried, teeth cleaned, and put to BED! But what happened to the radio? Where's the cat? The comics? There's so much going on. Why am I in a dark room fully washed and in pajamas? Help! Someone help! I'm being held captive in dark room and they're telling me I have to STAY there!

My only solution to this confining state when I was seven years old would be to march downstairs in segments of three separate trips.

First trip: 8:45 P.M. "Just to get a glass of water," I'd say. "I like the water down here instead of the water in the bathroom upstairs." The parents only found this slightly humorous. I go back to bed.

Second trip downstairs: 9:30. "Just checking to see that you two are OK. Things are OK upstairs, too." They don't see the humor in this. GET TO BED! (I now wonder if I ever interrupted their love life. Maybe I could have had another brother or sister if I'd left them alone in the late evening.)

But my main concern was that I wasn't tired and they put me to bed.

How come they get to stay up and I don't?

Third trip downstairs. It's 11:00 P.M. and wonderful classical music is coming out of the radio or record player. My parents, in the living room, are reading comfortably and looking semi-content that they've got things in their household under control.

By now they've had it with my antics; so the time has come when I can march straight through the living room, not even announce that I'm getting another glass of water from the kitchen, and I can walk back through the living room again on my way back upstairs. Their eyes follow me, they've seen this maneuver before, and no one says anything. I go upstairs to bed, and am asleep at midnight.

Then at six someone is saying, "It's time to go to school." I say to myself, "This is not the time to do anything. this is the time to go to sleep."

The sleep situation seems clear to me. You want to be awake at a certain time, and you want to sleep at a certain time. It should be the time *we* want to do these things. Why must we jump to someone else's drum when it comes to our sleep time?

I know there are certain things in life we have to follow called "rules of the road." If we don't get up and get going, forget it, life's a mess. The only thing I don't understand about the rules of the road of sleeping is: why can't the business day start a little later than eight or nine in the morning? It seems so frantic to scurry around at those hours when we're still half baked. Rushing is not one of my favorite things to do.

When I'm invited to friends' summer houses or vacation places for a weekend, I say to myself, "Ah, how great, I can sleep!" I tell the friends that I look forward to sleeping late in the wonderful air of the mountain top or by the sandy seashore, accompanied by the faint chirps of birds, waving tree branches, or the soft sloshing of waves.

They agree with me. Yes, this is the perfect place to sleep and unwind, it's just what you need. I think what wonderful friends they are.

Then reality sets in. When I get there, it seems it's an altogether different ballgame.

I mentioned to one couple how pleased I was that they understood that I like to sleep late on weekends. (I had explained this to them during the phone call when they invited me.) They nodded agreement, yes, yes, to my explanation, of course, that's exactly what one should do at a vacation house, rest.

I thought I'd reiterate my situation that I *really* sleep late on weekends, so they wouldn't worry when I didn't come out in the living room or kitchen at an early hour. The wife of the couple said, "Well, how late do you sleep?" I said I really couldn't say, it's just when the body decides to wake up. Sometimes it's eleven, sometimes noon, sometimes even one o'clock in the afternoon.

The wife had total shock on her face. She was trying to be charming as she laughed a lilting little laugh and told me she really didn't believe this. I said, "Yes, that's why I always bring it up when I'm invited to people's vacation houses on the weekend. It's a necessity that I catch up on my sleep."

My friend was still shocked and she said, "Well, Edan, we consider getting up anytime after eleven o'clock as *obscene!*"

We all laughed, ha ha, but I could see it in their eyes. They meant it.

When I went to bed that night, all I could do was stare wide-eyed at the ceiling and say to myself: "Anything after eleven o'clock is obscene." I thrashed around and it was hard to go to sleep.

Wouldn't you know it. I was also thrashing around in the early morning hours, too. I heard clattering going on in the kitchen at eight o'clock, which ordinarily doesn't wake me at all. (Only the noise from a jet engine one foot away from my ear, or noises of dynamite-blasting calibre, can wake me in the morning.)

Well, limp as an overcooked noodle, I clambered out of bed at 10:55. I dragged my bleary, bathrobed body into the kitchen and said, "Well, Lillian, I got up 'Five Minutes to Obscene.'" I thought they'd laugh and say, "Oh, you shouldn't have done that. We were joking last night. You could have stayed in bed." Instead, what they said was, "Wonderful! That's the way it should be! Aren't you glad you're up now so we can take brisk walks and go out and see a lot of things?"

I smiled. I ate my scrambled eggs. I knew I could not reach them with my perfect logic about sleeping.

At another friend's vacation home, I made the whole point clear a week before I arrived, just as in the above case. In addition, the night before we were to wake up on the first day, I explained it again. I like to sleep late — till maybe one o'clock in the afternoon. Total agreement.

Ah, I thought, now this time I'll *really* sleep.

Instead, what happened, starting at 10:00 A.M., was the sound of my hostess tapping on my bedroom door. "Are you all right?" "Yes, I'm all right. Remember last night when I told you I like to sleep late on weekends?"

Then twenty minutes later, another tap: "Are you *sure* you're all right? Is there anything I can bring you?" This knocking on the door continued until eleven, again the witching hour, when I finally gave up the fight and straggled out into the living room. My vacation place hostess exclaimed, "Oh, I'm so glad you're up! I was so worried about you — I thought maybe you were sick — but now you're up and that's good because now we can get going and see a lot of things!"

I smiled, ate my scrambled eggs, and knew that my logic about sleeping again was lost.

There are some people who don't wake me up when I'm visiting, even if I sleep until one o'clock in the afternoon. One set is my cousins in Florida who have no qualms about my sleeping; they go about their business, go out grocery shopping and do all sorts of errands — and they don't care that I sleep late. Also, when I'm on vacation and visiting my mother, it's a definite agreement that my sleeping late is something she'll go along with. At one point she even said, "Maybe you've been right all these years. Except for getting up to go to school or going to work, maybe people in their free time should sleep the way they want to."

There are definite events we must wake up for, so I'm not saying we should sleep willy-nilly and irresponsibly.

THE TEN THINGS IN LIFE WE MUST WAKE UP FOR

1. To go to a job.
2. To go to school.
3. To get the car registered.
4. To catch a bus, plane, or train.
5. To keep an early morning appointment with a dentist, doctor, lawyer, or accountant.
6. Worse yet, to go to an early morning appointment with the IRS.
7. To feed the cat or to take the dog out.
8. To take care of an emergency.
9. To go to an early religious or funeral service.
10. To make a call to friends in Australia. (Their time zone is the opposite of ours, and you want to make sure that your call gets to them at a reasonable hour of day or night.)

These are the only times that I encourage anyone to snap out of bed. The rest of the time, I say the body should wake up when it wants to.

Whenever I can, I like to wake up at the crack of noon.

Then there's the trap we all know about — too much sleep, which makes us unbelievably drowsy the rest of the day. We've let the body overindulge, and this I'm not advocating. I'm talking about just the right amount of sleep. The body knows the right amount of sleep it needs — all we have to do is listen to the messages we receive: "Hello, Person? This is the body speaking. Please give me eight or nine hours of sleep tonight. I've had a busy week and I'm pooped. Thanks. Over and out. Your friend, the body."

So as people living alone, whenever the body feels like a nap, a snooze, or a long sleep, go along with it. If you've been into a lot of things lately, e.g., work-wise, project-wise, social-wise, sports-wise, conscientious citizen-wise, your body wants to pause and regroup.

Then there's always the situation of just plain languishing. To languish is a wonderful thing, and people living alone should take advantage of this. When I say languish, I don't mean sixteen hours in an easy chair in front of the TV with beer cans and potato chip bags strewn around the floor. Languishing as a sophisticated person living alone takes a certain amount of time and effort.

To languish is an art. First of all, you'll want to obtain the softest, most comfortable bed and couch that you can. (Even if you get a firm mattress, make the rest of the bed soft and inviting.) Make your bed exactly as you want it to be in the way of comforters, blankets, your just-right colors, the exact number and fluffiness of pillows — firm, semi-firm, medium, and soft.

Let's say everything is just as it should be in your couch and bed areas. One day at 2:30 in the afternoon, for no reason, you really feel like curling up with a bunch of soft pillows to take a nap. This is *not* the time to think, "Oh, no. I can't do that. Sleeping at 2:30 in the afternoon is something only sloths do."

Go to your one hundred percent wonderful bed and languish and stretch and drift in and out of sleep, just as a cat does. Squeeze every last drop out of this luxury you have as a person who lives alone and happens to be home at 2:30 P.M. and wants to sleep.

Now about weekends. I, as an Owl, encourage sleeping late to catch up from the past week. This means not answering the phone on Saturday and Sunday mornings until at least 11:00 A.M. If you've already told friends that this is your quirk, you know that anyone who's calling you at 9:00 A.M. on Sunday is someone you don't know.

The solution is either 1) get an answering machine or 2) in your half-sleep simply count the rings of the telephone...one, two... three...up to eleven or thirteen (or however many the person who is calling decides to let it ring) and then drift back to sleep. If you count the rings, it makes you feel like you're "doing something," yet it won't stir you to put one foot out of the bed. Putting one foot out of the bed (when you want to sleep) is deadly. One foot only leads to another foot out, and pretty soon you'll be awake. This is not what we want when our first preference is to sleep.

So when you're languishing (stretching out luxuriously during any time of the day or night), make it a production.

Yawn, stretch your legs, make a yawning *noise,* and curl around pillows. Your languish time is important. It makes you feel incredibly successful and in control of the time in your life. Languishing — stretching, coiling up, napping, with *no guilt,* is amazingly energizing. In most cases, you'll bounce off your great couch or bed and tackle more projects than you ever thought you could.

And as far as sleep goes, you get an added feature: "Home Movies of the Mind," which we commonly call Dreams.

Dreams are one of the best ways of getting messages *from* yourself *to* yourself. They are usually what you *actually* have swirling through your mind, as opposed to the things you think about during your waking hours.

For example, during the time you're awake you might be thinking, "I try to do a good job...I work so hard...I wish things would work out better for me... why can't I make more money...what bus do I take to get from Point A to Point B...who's that good-looking person standing over there...what should I have for lunch."

That night you have two or three dreams that you remember. One was that you were walking along some glorious countryside and you saw a group of people you know having a picnic. They wave you over, and as you almost get to where they are, you back off, saying to yourself, "They don't really want me. Who wants to be with those people, anyway." The next dream might be that you've been asked to enter some artwork in an art showing. (In real life you don't even paint, but that's the way dreams go.) You bring some of your well-executed and very professional paintings to the gallery. But as you near it, you say to yourself, "They'll probably put these in a dusty corner and no one will see them. Why should I give my paintings to a gallery that will do that." And you turn around and go home.

If you continue to have dreams where something good is about to happen until you pour cold water on it, try to think how this relates to what you do in waking life. It could be that when something positive has happened, you might verbally say to a friend, "Oh, they gave me a big office, but this company is so crazy they might take it away from me and give it to someone else six months from now." (In reality, companies usually do not boot people out of offices that have been assigned to them, but you have your own erroneous reasoning going on, planted there from who-knows-where.) Or, again in waking life, you might be invited to a sensational party, but you hear yourself saying, "I won't find anyone to talk to. Those people will probably be phonies." You should be getting a clue by now that what your dreams are telling you by their stories is what you're *thinking* consciously.

The dream doesn't care what kind of visuals it has to use — it'll pick anything, jet plants, monsters, art galleries, gooey mud that keeps you from running swiftly, wonderful things, and frightening things, relatives, friends, acquaintances, celebrities and strangers.

In the case of the sample dreams mentioned, the stories of the people at the picnic in the country and the gallery invitation — where you poured cold water on both — possibly are prompting you to ask yourself: "Do I do that in waking life?" It might show you a part of yourself that you just weren't aware of.

Some people keep records of their dreams by writing them in a notebook the next day. Over the months they can see a pattern emerge.

Your dream thoughts are just as real as what goes on during your waking hours. As one-person householders, I say we might as well take advantage of any scraps of information that come our way that can give us some insight into what makes us tick. Western Union delivers messages, so do dreams.

So catch as many Z's as you want, and dream away.

To sum up, simply remember that one of the Basic Rights of a one-person householder is to sleep and catnap whenever you want — free of any guilty feelings, and without interruption — *anytime* of the day or night that you choose.

Sleep wasn't invented for no reason, it was meant to be enjoyed to the hilt.

11 *Your Friends. The Best Thing Ever Invented*

Friends are different from any other people in your life.

They're not related to you. They're not holding a lot of emotional baggage over your head from childhood or from any other historical phase of your life.

They could be, but usually are not, your employer, so they're not holding the golden paycheck that insures you have a roof over your head and weekly groceries.

They're not acquaintances whom you can more or less do without — as well as their being able to do without you.

They're not strangers in the night who find you charming only for a while and then move on.

They're not hail and farewell types who slap you on the back, tell you that you're the most terrific person they've ever met, and then the next day can't even remember your name when they see you on the street.

The people we're talking about are the good old-fashioned garden variety: SOLID FRIENDS who go through many aspects of life with you, and you with them.

For a person living alone, they're the most important thing in your life. These are people you *choose* to have around you. Without friends, you might as well give up on living alone, because you'll never make it without them.

There's no denying that relatives can be as helpful and wonderful as all get out, and probably you have some you consider friends, too. But they're not the same as non-relative friends who look you straight in the eye and level with you from a peer's point of view. Friends are people you can open up with one hundred percent.

Friends can come in many varieties and they don't have to live exactly as you live. They can be married people, single people,

people older then you, or younger than you, people living three or ten thousand miles away, or someone living right next door. Why it works this way, I don't know. It seems we can sometimes meet someone we feel we have known all our lives, and time, distance, and life status doesn't have anything to do with the great friendship that develops.

There is a genuine warmth that flows from friends. It tells you they are on your side. You would take them on your lifeboat any day. You can trust them. And as much as they seem to add to your life, you add a lot to their lives, too. Friends are special.

I'll say without qualification that on my road to becoming semi-charming, non-broke, and somewhat together, I'd hand most of the thanks to friends who listened to me over the years.

I've had my best laughs with friends about the oddities of life, and I've soaked their shoulders with tears about life in general and daily life in particular.

I'll never forget how those shoulders felt as they supported me. As odd as it seems, I'd sometimes make sure the person wasn't wearing a jacket with shoulder pads — I didn't want to produce soggy pads due to talking about my life and all its ramifications.

The first time I began to see the intense value of a person as a friend was when I was working my way through college and at one point needed $200 for tuition for one more semester. I fussed and fumed. I knew I couldn't add another job to my existing part-time jobs to get the money. I mentally went through everyone I knew — friends and relatives — and my thoughts went to a friend in a nearby city. I remembered him as being especially sincere and kind.

I took a deep breath and picked up the phone. This was the first time I'd ever asked for a loan from anyone. My friend answered the phone and was glad to hear from me, but before we got into any chit-chat, I said, "Ken, I don't know what to do. I've got to get $200 more to pay my next semester's tuition...and..."

He cut me off right there and said, "It's being sent to you in the next few minutes by Western Union. It's yours." I couldn't believe my ears. I shouted, laughed, and cried all at once, then said, very businesslike, "This is a loan, and I'll mail you an agreement with terms and interest." He said, "Fine, fine, whatever you say."

The incident jolted me into a whole new world. What a beautiful thing a friend is as a support system.

Now, I don't know what would have happened if I'd asked for

$5,000. I have a suspicion that this is not the right thing to ask from a friend. A friendship is a fragile thing and it's not equipped to handle mega-requests unless all the details surrounding the situation stack up properly.

One of the best things about friends is that they don't have to be perfect, and neither do you. You can have a friend who's terrific in most ways, but has one funny quirk that nips on your nerves. What do you do? You ignore it. Since you don't spend twenty-four hours of every day with the friend, what's the difference if she or he has an irritating quirk or two? There's so much you like about the person, and that's the part you care about. They, in turn, will be glad to overlook your one tiny imperfection, too.

When I think of what *my* friends overlook in me, my mind boggles. I get grumpy and sullen when life isn't going right. When I'm thinking hard, I get a mean expression on my face. I get impatient when things don't happen NOW.

Also, in humid weather my hair frizzes and locks of it shaped like wings spring out of my head.

I thank my friends that they don't mind talking to someone who looks like a Brillo pad with wings.

Luckily, it's not only the surface they're talking to, they're talking to the whole me.

I commend friends for putting up with my psychological and physical shortcomings. I try to work on my failings, mostly by talking about them with friends — who help me just by sincerely listening and caring.

Listening, of course, is a two-way street. You can't always be the talker, you also want to reciprocate and listen genuinely to your friend. It's a fifty-fifty proposition.

The benefits and joys I've derived from friends are endless. I wish I could go up to them and hug their necks this very minute to thank them for what they've done for me.

Friends make us feel worthwhile.

After college when I first went out in the world, I, through a series of incidents, didn't think I was any great shakes as a human being. But through pounding and pounding of good words from friends, I began to believe that, OK, maybe I am a fairly nice person after all.

Friends are with us and understand us when we're down in the dumps (for a short period of time, not forever).

Friends will help us out in an emergency.

Friends feel as good as we do when we have successful things happen to us. They're the ones who have helped us get there.

There's a saying, "When I'm a winner, everyone wins."

Friends are on "your side" when you tell them about something rotten that happened to you at work or in dealing with other people.

If something went wrong, it must have been the other people who caused it, not you. You're their pal, and they support you through the crushing waves of life. They like you, they want you around, and you can add something to their lives, so they'll do all they can to keep you afloat.

Friends also, in gentle ways, let you know when you're being a phony. Good friends act as a "mirror" to you. A mirror doesn't lie, it tells it like it is. Friends won't let you get away with being dishonest, and it's one of the best things about them.

Friendship isn't a mushy-wushy kind of thing — it's as honest and direct and nurturing a relationship as ever was invented.

They don't psychologically club you down with nitpicking about your faults. A friendship is a very sensitive thing, and topics are dealt with in the same manner that porcupines make love: carefully.

Now, there's also "The Shifting Sands of Friendships." People and friendships can change with time. Your best friend in high school won't necessarily be your best friend twenty years later. Your great pal from last year may even have done something to make you want to dissolve the friendship or temporarily put it "on hold." And at times people may want to do that to you, too. You're simply not on the same wavelength anymore.

It's hard to break a friendship that you thought would last forever. But if it's not working, let it go.

When people drop me as a friend, I reluctantly accept it. Many times people give and get out of a friendship what they need at a certain time, and then they move on.

I've made a pact with myself not to take a negative gloom-and-doom person on as a friend. A negative person is an energy vampire. And who knows, they may enjoy being the way they are, and my tendency would be to try to change them. So I leave them be, and I'm sure they don't miss me.

To summarize the subject of friends, they make you stretch and grow; they listen to your good news and your bad news; they like you because you listen to their news; they're not hostile; they pick you up when you feel bad and they don't berate you when you make a mistake; they're not out to get you for some past contretemps; they like you for the way you are; and they want to help.

Nothing in my adult life would have happened as positively as it did unless I had friends who helped me from one phase to another.

Friends: I couldn't get anywhere without 'em.

The Luxury of Being Alone When You Want to Plan, Plot, and Hatch Your Ideas

12

There's a definite luxury to having time by yourself.

Let's say your life is filled with enough social life, classes, and work and other activities that may supply you with income. Let's also say you're working on several projects that interest you, and you seem to be doing a lot of running around. In fact, you're going around in so many circles you're beginning to get a little frazzled around the edges.

It's time to be by yourself to recoup and regroup.

First of all, think how lucky you are to be able to pick and choose the time you want to have by yourself. *No one* is standing there telling you that you must do something else instead.

There's a wonderful aspect to time by yourself. You can treat yourself to anything and everything that's special to you. It could be reading fabulous or trashy books; giving your cat, dog, goldfish, or canary the undivided attention you like to give them; soaking in a tub of perfect-temperature water; making phone calls to people who add comfort and warmth to your life; eating every favorite food you can think of (within reason); doing some of your favorite exercises; listening to the radio, to self-help cassette tapes, or to favorite records; watching TV or movies and other programs on a VCR. The list is endless.

Under no circumstances are you to feel like you're a terrible and selfish person because you are doing the things you want to do. Living alone, you have a disadvantage or two that other people don't have. So when a luxury like spending quality time on yourself comes along, luxuriate in it and apologize to no one. You are doing your best in the outside world and have given a lot of yourself to others, and now it's your turn.

A friend of mine says he has a few friends who tell him he has life too easy living alone, because he can do what he wants, see whom he wants to, and generally can live high on the hog with no thought to others. He says these are mostly married men, and he feels they're trying to make him feel a tad guilty. It's possible that they're envious of him and want to goad him a little.

I suggested he keep those friends at arm's length. Unless their situations change, and they all of a sudden develop wonderful home lives of their own, they're going to continue to nip at him. He agreed and sees less of them now.

He didn't need to be told he was against Mom, Apple Pie, and the American Way just because he enjoyed life living alone at the moment.

So let's look at what happens during the time you want to be absolutely by yourself.

During the time you want to be alone, you don't have to:

1. Look presentable.
2. Worry about when someone's coming home.
3. Answer the phone.
4. Close any door in the house for privacy.
5. Fix food for anyone.
6. Do chores.
7. Clean up after anyone.
8. Listen or talk to anyone.
9. Go somewhere with anyone.
10. Be charming.

You've said, OK world, I think I've had enough for a while. So you come home, put on your most comfortable duds, and contemplate any subject that suits your fancy.

You feel nothing better could happen to you than this time when you and yourself are going to commune.

After all, by this time, you've worked on yourself so that you're a fairly nice human being and you really enjoy your own company.

You're not bitter, mean, sarcastic, grumpy, or a big bore. You're an interesting person to be with. You enjoy your own company.

Even if Paul Newman or Sophia Loren knocked on the door to come visit you, you might politely ask them to come by another time.

This is your time alone.

The important thing is that it's not down-in-the-dumps time, or feel-sorry-for-yourself time, or you-just-don't-have-anything-else-to-do time. It's *quality* time spent to rejuvenate yourself.

I don't know why, but I always start quality time alone by reading the day's newspaper. I guess it's my "decompression" time in leaving the outside world behind me.

The next thing I'll do is stare into space (but not for more than fifteen minutes) to figure out what I want to do.

I usually decide to take a nap amongst all my soft and snazzy pillows. I figure this will leave me rested and in better shape to think about what to do.

Then getting up and feeling more invigorated, the next thing I do is get out a pad of ruled paper and make a list. I'll put down everything from the ridiculous to the sublime including:

1. How to make myself more attractive.
2. What new classes I should take.
3. How to meet more people of the opposite sex.
4. Books I want to read.
5. Vacations I want to go on.
6. How to fix up my wardrobe.
7. What to do to make the world a better place. Which senators to write to.
8. My money situation — income and outgo.
9. Things to fix up in the house.
10. Make a list of my strong points and my weak points and work on the latter.

There's something so comforting about a list. It makes you feel you've got your flotsam and jetsam in control. Even if you don't do half the things on the list, you'll at least feel you have a grip on your circumstances.

Who knows, maybe Michelangelo did it too:

1. Get the plaster.
2. Get the water to mix with the plaster.
3. Think of a good idea.
4. Make a sculpture.

The theory says it's the writing down, not the thinking, that gets things done. You're visualizing what you want to happen as you write.

Then there's the best thing about writing lists: crossing things off. It's even more interesting to use a yellow felt pen and highlight the things you've accomplished. This gives you a pat on the back. You're a person who gets things done. It's highlighted right there in front of you. You're a terrific person.

There is another kind of list to make in your quality alone time: a Wish List.

There's a saying, What a person can conceive, a person can achieve. So conceive big things and write them down. Split the list in two parts:

WISH LISTS

1. List the things you're willing to spend time, money, and energy on getting. This can be anything: a new car, a new wardrobe, a redecorated house, a new job, improvement at a sport or skill, a better lawn, more involvement in helping other people when your abilities can really add something.

2. A list of "everything" you've ever wanted, and the sky's the limit: a trip to Europe, a luxury-liner cruise around the world, millions of dollars a year in income, the perfect mate, the perfect job, the perfect outlet for your specialized talents. Who knows, they could happen, and it's fun to think about them.

What does it cost to make such lists? Nothing, except the lead in the pencil and the price of two pieces of paper. And, interestingly enough, you'll soon find that you start to make things actually happen that you've put on the lists.

What have you accomplished by spending some time alone?

1. You've stopped your heavy duty finagling with all the "have to's" in your life.

2. You feel you have control over day-to-day and long-term items by writing them down.

3. You have done luxurious things.

4. You've thought about how to improve your life (again).

5. You've planned for things you want to achieve.

6. You've written down a "Christmas list" of all the wishes you've ever had — a most pleasant way to spend time.

During all of these activities, you haven't overtaxed yourself. It doesn't take much energy to make a list, sleep among comfortable pillows, sit in a perfect-temperature tub of water, eat your favorite foods, or read a juicy book.

Can you imagine how good your attitude will be when you reenter the outside world in your bathed, well-rested, and refreshed body and mind?

Ah. What good stuff comes out of quality time alone.

13 The Art of Having Visitors When You Want Them

There are two schools of thought about visitors: let them drop by whenever they feel like it, unannounced; or, make a plan ahead of time as to when they'll come over, for what, and for how long — an hour? Two hours? An afternoon? An evening? A week? A year?

When we live alone, we begin to realize we have space and time for ourselves, and it's important how we use it.

I'm not saying we should be Mr. or Ms. Pennygrinch and rarely open our doors to visitors. Never. All I know is that it pays off in the long run to plan for and space visitors.

Why? Because you want to chop up your time to make it work in your favor. You're the commander of your one-person householder's ship, and too many unexpected doorbell rings get the ship off course.

It may be entirely different in a bustling household with six kids. The telephone is forever ringing and the doorbell is being pushed by a guy on the other side who's wearing a baseball glove and waiting to play with Tommy. Or Aunt Jessica drives by and sees that your car is in the driveway, so she knew you were home, and only wants to stop in for a minute and say hello.

I'm sure this family has some sort of schedule for getting things done, even though unexpected visitors are dropping by all day, and things work out fine.

There are people I know who live either in the suburbs or the city who are glad to throw open the door and welcome anyone who's standing there. It works for them. But my one-person household goes off-tilt if it's broken up with unexpected visitors. It breaks up what I'm trying to accomplish, no matter what it might be.

There's a rhythm that my weeks have: go to work, come home,

go to social events, have social events at my house, work on projects. The only way I can get any of these things done is with a certain degree of planning.

This doesn't rule out spontaneity or that most pleasurable of things, serendipity — when you stumble on a wonderful thing unexpectedly.

Planning is definitely not meant to make you anti-social.

What if Mr. X shows up when you've got Mr. Z in the house and you're right in the middle of a hot and heavy game of chess. Would Mr. X be welcome? Not by me he wouldn't. I like Mr. X, but he's watering down my special time with Mr. Z.

What if you've looked forward all day to some activity in the evening, even watching "Casablanca" for the hundredth time on TV, and Parson Brown comes by and wants to chat for three hours. We know he means well, he thinks it's his job, but what's wrong with a simple pre-arrangement of the visit?

You're there to welcome people when you and they have arranged it. Making plans for visits for specific reasons makes them special. What are you, an old shoe that anyone can step on? No. You're a person doing interesting things, and your life and time are important to you. And your good friends will understand this.

When I'm at someone's house and they have the "no-plan" policy of visitors, I'm astounded at what happens. We might be sitting down to dinner and having the most soul-searching, intricate, and interesting conversation. Then there's a knock on the door. People want to come in and visit. They already had dinner, so they pull up chairs by the table and watch us eat. They're not that interested in the topic we were talking about, so we go to a topic they like.

To me, the person who has the no-plan policy is just sitting there for everyone's whim. If they don't mind, OK. I just don't get it.

These people also can't imagine that *I plan* to have people over. They think my policy is odd.

Whatever works, I say.

Then there are unsolicited phone calls, the worst thing ever invented, called "telemarketing": a euphemism for phone calls from people you don't want to hear from, who are trying to sell you something you don't want to buy.

When my phone rings, I like to think it's someone calling to tell me that my ship or their ship has finally come in. Or it's Mr. Right calling. Or it's a friend inviting me to a dinner party. Or an organization telling me my artistic/writing talents are just what they want, and when can I come down and pick up my million dollar check.

OK. It's not one of these calls. It's someone trying to sell me something.

My policy is to say pleasantly, I'm not interested, but thank you for calling. Then I hang up.

I hear the person catch his or her breath. They're so grateful someone actually thanked them for calling!

What a job those telephone solicitors have. I don't envy what they do, and I wish them well. But they're unwelcome visitors in my single-person household where I expect important or comforting things as a result of the phone ringing.

No matter what your phone-call and in-person visitor policies are at the moment, I highly recommend that you review them every once in a while.

Lots of company comes over to my place, and we have a pretty good time. And I go to lots of other people's houses, and we have a pretty good time.

We have a simple, basic policy:

1. Call.
2. Pick a day.
3. Pick a time.
4. Decide what the point of the visit is. Just to say hello? Fine. Work on a project? Fine. Eat dinner and discuss life in general? Fine.

You won't be thought of as cold-hearted because you have a planned-visitor policy. People will understand. They'll feel both they and you are special for setting aside time for a get-together.

Visitors. I love 'em when I expect them!

Pets. They Love You When You're Happy, and They Comfort You When You're Not

14

I'll state my position about pets: I'm a pushover for them.

There's something special about a pet living in a one-person household.

A pet in most households is usually well-liked, even adored, and is one of the family.

But the pet who is owned by a person living alone is a star. The pet gets much more individualized attention from us.

I've been partial to pets and furry creatures ever since I was a toddler and would walk up to the most menacing dog on the street and give him a lick of my ice cream cone. Many fierce-looking dogs were awfully surprised to get ice cream out of the blue when I came along, and there was a lot of tail wagging that ensued. This tactic gave my parents a few gray hairs and heart palpitations, but it didn't stop me from meandering down the street giving any food I had to any animal. I saw no bad in any of them, they were all my pals.

I was comfortable with animals as a child because we had gentle dogs as pets from the time I can remember.

Even if a pet got cranky because I'd tousle its ear and it didn't feel like playing and rollicking about, I'd say to myself, "That's OK. Maybe some other time." I learned the live-and-let-live philosophy at a young age from pets.

Pets can help us through so many of the lumps of living alone, and those who have pets know exactly what I mean.

Sometimes, we feel that it's not the right time, for whatever reason, to have a pet. Perfectly understandable. One of the best things about living alone is freedom, including not having to take care of anything else. I've gone through phases where I was pet-less, and it's worked to my advantage at the time.

At those times I'll fill the need for a pet by volunteering to take care of someone else's cat or dog at my place while they're out of town. It works out fine. I get pet companionship, but I'm not committed for a long period of time, and the friend is happy not to put Fluffy or Roscoe in a kennel. Also, the pet is happy getting my attention and a change of scenery.

But back to pet ownership, here are the pluses most of us have experienced.

The pet:

1. Is always waiting with joy when we come home.
2. Shows so much adoration to us through its eyes. (This is the part that melts us.)
3. Rearranges its life around our comings and goings.
4. Makes cheerful noises — meows, barks, or chirps. (Sometimes too early in the morning for my liking. Pets are great getter-uppers at 6:00 A.M. — wanting breakfast and ready to play.)
5. Is soft, furry, cuddly, and will sponge up all the love we send its way.
6. Provides us with unbelievable antics and entertainment.

Realistically speaking, there are disadvantages about having pets — you clean up after them, they whine, they can disrupt a household. The same things can be said about having children, yet people continue to have them, and people will continue to have pets in their households, too. The positives outweigh the negatives.

A trap regarding pets that people can easily fall into when they're living alone is letting one's whole life revolve around the pet. How do I know? Because I've done it. We make the pet "It."

Don't exclude lots of people because you think life is complete by having a pet.

Pets *and* people are the right combination to have in your life.

Also, no matter how satisfying it is to talk hour after hour with your pet, we must understand they're not reciprocating with us, talk-wise. Communication-wise, yes; words, no. The pet is *not* human. There's a lot of communication going on, but you're the person and they're still the pet.

Who goes out in the rain and wind and goes to the job and gets the money and goes to the store and gets the food for the two of you? Who pays the rent? Who cleans the place? In your mind, you must *know* who's the owner and who's the pet. (This is hard for me. Many times I've had the feeling that they're the boss, and I'm just their servant going out and working to have money enough to bring them good stuff for the supermarket or pet store.)

The final chapter of owning a pet, its death, through sickness or from natural old age, to me, is almost unbearable.

I think a person living alone gets hit harder and goes more emotionally berserk when a pet dies.

We've invested so much one-to-one energy, soul, and heart in the animal, and it in us. There's a special bond. We've been room-mates for years. We've gone through every grim and glorious detail of life together. We've been the closest of buddies. We've inun-dated each other with our lumps and happy times. We've cried and laughed and romped around for years.

There's one thing I suggest after the death of your pet and dur-ing the time you're grieving over your loss: don't spend time or talk to anyone who's anti-animal. They'll say, "Oh, what's an old dog — how can you be so sad over just an animal? Snap out of it."

Frankly, when I've had pets die, I couldn't even make it to work the next day. It's taken me months to "snap out of it," and it's a few years before I can condition myself to say I'm ready for a pet again.

The hurt of losing a pet is an emotion that goes through me like a knife.

Once, when a pet cat died of normal old age, I again had these strong reactions and decided I didn't want to go through another pet routine for a long time. Five years went by, and I said, "I can't stand not having a pet again."

Some friends had what I thought was a solution. They had two beautiful lovebirds in an equally beautiful ornate and large birdcage sitting to one side of their elegant living room. I thought to myself, "That's the answer. I'll get two birds, they'll be in the corner and chirp, and that will be that; I can't possibly get involved."

The first day I brought home two little white parakeets and a beautiful ornate cage, I was calm and OK.

The second day, I gave them names, Cynthia and Charlie. One looked more elegant and snooty than the other, and that was Cynthia. The guy with the big eyes I named Charlie.

The third day I was going up to the ornate cage every half hour and observing their two distinct personalities. One haughty, one lovey-dovey.

The first month, I was hooked. I and company that came by had such great times analyzing Charlie and Cynthia and putting on their favorite music: opera. And there were flying-around times in the living room, and great times out on the terrace.

Charlie tried to be friendly to Cynthia by nuzzling up to her, but she would brush him off with a haughty look. He never got discouraged. Her eyes were misty, gray, and cold. She kept them half-closed as she glared at him. Charlie's eyes were black, warm, and wide open. He adored Cynthia.

We had our rituals established. Every night we would have flying-around time. The chirping was almost deafening as I opened their cage and they flew from lamp to lamp to the tops of framed pictures.

Even Cynthia had a ball outside of the cage. But back inside again, she put all her rules and regulations into effect. She got to eat first; she got the best perch; she got to peck at the celery first. Charlie always had to play second fiddle. Still, he always looked at her admiringly. He didn't want much from her, just to be her friend. I don't know how he could have stood to be her lackey for as long as he lived.

Within a year, we had a lifestyle going for us, a perfect pets and owner situation. They were happy, and so was I.

In the summers, they'd spend time out on the terrace in their cage, getting sun and fine mist baths from the garden hose as I watered the plants and trees. They'd also get lots of visits from neighborhood sparrows who came up for seeds I left out. Life was generally pretty good.

It was a fascinating experience owning them. When they died after almost eleven years, I thought my heart would break. Charlie died first, leaving cold-hearted Cynthia and me together. We tried to hit it off, but she wasn't very interested when I'd try to talk and communicate with her. She was bewildered at first when Charlie had gone, but she got over it in a hurry when it dawned on her that she finally had the cage all to herself.

As long as someone kept her place clean and kept seeds and celery and lettuce coming in, she was fine. That was all she needed. She cleaned and preened her feathers constantly, luxuriating in her "Cynthia-ness."

We had a glorious eleven years together, and when they died, the vet said he'd never had a case of housebound birds living so long. He said they were exceptionally well cared for pets.

And I said when I got them there was no way I would get involved. I had eleven years of involvement, and loved it. I don't feel odd about my feelings. I wasn't excluding taking care of people at the same time. The pets nourished me to get out of the house and do as much as I could for people.

I'm nuts about pets and living creatures of all kinds. Animals continue to be some of my best friends.

The huffy looking Persian cat on the about the author page helped me stay awake until three and four in the morning when I was writing this book. She was always willing to purr loudly and give an ear for scratching whenever I needed a break.

There's one thing for us to remember about our one-person householder pet: we're out in the world doing all sorts of things with a lot of people. But from a pet's viewpoint, *we're* the only thing they have.

We're very important to them, these furry guys.

I'm thankful for the honesty and openness pets have taught me. There's one thing about them — they can sniff out a phony immediately. Either you like them and are comfortable with them or you're not. No in between.

To those of you who don't cotton-up to pets, I say that's OK.

But to the rest of us, I say love them as much as you want, but look out for the peril of devoting your whole existence to them. Keep humans coming and going in your life, too.

Humans are able to love you when you're happy and comfort when you're sad. But sometimes it takes humans a long time to find out how to do it.

Pets know automatically.

15 Grooming Habits. Keep Your Teeth & Nails Clean & the Seams of Your Clothes Sewn Together

What's one of the first things that goes by the wayside when no one is with us for a while?

Our appearance.

It's OK to look odd, messy, and downright ugly when in the house tidying up the birdcage or cleaning the oven with that foamy stuff that smells.

But when we step outside, we don't want to scare animals and little children by the way we look.

I've scared myself sometimes when I've glanced in the mirror after not caring how I look for a half day or so — wings sprouting from my hair; grimy; my face pasty-looking like pie dough; and on top of that, if I was thinking hard, I even had an angry, warlike expression on my face. I'd say to the mirror, "Where did *you* come from!?" Then I'd realize it was me.

To solve the problem, I'd make a point not to look in the mirror until I got myself cleaned up. Sometimes I'd take a peek, however, just to see how crummy I could really look.

There's nothing wrong with looking semi-sloppy and unkempt around the house. I'm sure married people and people living in other groups don't always look like Donna Reed or Robert Young on the TV show, "Father Knows Best."

Donna Reed ran up and down steps and did *all* her housework in high heels. And I think Robert Young wore his necktie to bed. I never saw him without it. She was beautifully coiffed, and he never needed a shave.

Unless grooming and looking beautiful or handsome every minute of the day is something that is second nature — there are people like this, and I aspire to be one of them — the rest of us one-person householders have to get into the habit of checking how we look before we sally forth into the outside world. We must also check our body bulges occasionally and get rid of them by exercising — even by walking more than usual. Body bulges in the wrong places are not sophisticated.

Being embarrassingly-groomed happens to others, too, but it's more apt to happen to us. We don't have someone to check us out before we open the front door.

Here are some rules to help avoid mortifying ourselves when we go out in public:

1. If you've just eaten breakfast, check to see there are no bits of egg or shredded wheat on your face or lips.

2. Specks of spinach or anything else between teeth tend to downgrade a winning smile from a ten to a zero. Brush or floss your teeth and get the specks out.

3. When you've brushed your teeth, check to see if you left white toothpaste at the sides of your mouth and the small top part of your chin. These are the places toothpaste likes to settle. You'll look like a mad dog if you don't remove it.

4. Are you wearing a garment that you meant to take to the cleaners? Does it have a spot where you dropped greasy pizza three weeks ago? Don't say, "Oh, it doesn't show." IT DOES.

5. Try to prevent foodstuffs from falling on prominent parts of your clothing or body. Once I saw a businessman in a fast-food restaurant eating chicken with his hands, but he had flipped his tie over his shoulder as he diligently chomped. I thought, "What a good idea. He's solving several problems at once: nothing will fall on the tie; if something falls on his shirt, he can put his tie over it when he's through eating, and; he won't have to walk around with a noticeable stain all day." Chances are nothing plopped on his shirt, but by tossing his tie over to his back, he had insurance in case anything did.

6. What about the lining of a coat that is drooping because the stitches came out of the hem? Are you going to walk out of your house with shiny satin fabric flapping along in the breeze at the bottom of your coat? Examine your coat every once in a while. Other people do.

7. What about seams in general? Do you know how often seams open up with abandon? In the most unlikely places? Seams are in almost every piece of clothing we have, and as people living alone,

somebody's got to watch them as they spring open, and that means us. Instead of adding angst to my life by looking for, finding, and using needle and thread to sew these things, I take the seams to the tailor at the dry cleaners. He knows what he's doing when it comes to seams.

8. Heels and backs of shoes — how often do you look at them? You'd be surprised at what's been going on back there. Cuts in the leather, scuffs, worn-down heels, and unusual debris.

9. If you have a hole in the back of your sock, the sock will rise up and the hole will show. If you have a hole in the toe of your sock, your big toe will protrude through it and you'll feel funny. Use the sock as a dust mitt instead.

10. Keep your clothes in a clean state. You're used to seeing them and putting them on every day. Your eye simply "doesn't see" when things have happened to them. Check a garment before you put it on for rips, dirt, and wrinkles. Your laundry room and your dry cleaning place should become second homes to you once you get in the habit of keeping everything clean, clean, clean — not only for the sake of the outside world that looks at you, but for your own sense of self-worth.

11. Is it time to send your three year old tennis or running shoes up to the big athletic field in the sky?

12. Why is lipstick on your front teeth and halfway up your cheek? Or, if you're a man, why is shaving cream and bits of toilet paper up there?

13. How did that dirt get under your nails? Get it out. Why are bits of fallen hair strands riding merrily on your shoulders throughout the day? Brush it off.

14. Cologne, men's and women's: you have to be your own tough judge on this. Don't forget the basic reason you're wearing it — to make yourself more attractive to people. Overkill does just the opposite. If the cat passes out as you walk by, you've got too much on. If people in the elevator reel and move their eyes to the skies, you've got too much on. Be sensitive to your scent dousings.

15. The most important thing you can acquire for yourself in your live-alone state is a good full-length mirror. It will help keep you from going out of the house with something embarrassing hanging from you.

The degree to which I groom myself depends on where I'm going:

- To take out the garbage.
- To the supermarket.
- To work.
- To meet a person who might be Mr. Right.
- To a snazzy party at Mrs. Astor's residence...with Mr. Right.

Now, there's one point about grooming that doesn't work. *Over*-grooming and, in haste, remaking yourself so you don't even remotely resemble the real you.

This happened to me twice — before a trip to South America to see the Amazon River and before a vacation to London. I went to beauty parlors before leaving on each of these trips and asked them to do something special to my hair. Did they ever! Indians in the South American jungles and conservative Londoners leaped backwards when they saw me coming. (But once they found the real me under the hairdos, everything worked out fine and I had good times.) Since then, I never get anything "special" done before I go on a trip, and I'm much more comfortable.

All we have to remember about grooming is not to under-do it and not to overdo it.

I'm still concentrating on coming out of the house every day with my hair sprigs and body parts under control so I can really have a successful day.

Some people take to good grooming naturally. They always look as though they just stepped out of a beautiful magazine ad.

Many articles have been written about these people. In 100°, high humidity weather, they don't even perspire. A hair is never out of line, clothes stay unwrinkled throughout the day, shoes maintain their perfect shine, shirts are immaculately crisp, and nothing falls out of place.

I don't understand how these people do it. When I stand next to one of them, I all of a sudden see an open seam on the sleeve of my blouse, a scuff mark on the toe of my shoe, and a curious mark on the hem of my skirt from a taxi door I slammed on it earlier in the day.

I work on grooming habits every day, but there always seem to be forces working against me. I'll continue to try to improve.

My problem might have started from childhood when I was awakened abruptly and didn't have time or the energy to do things properly before leaving for school. I'm still dressing in a rush in the morning, and this does not make for a crisp-looking person.

Some of my best-groomed friends tell me they spend one to two hours in the morning getting ready. This kind of time allocation does not fit into my schedule.

I search for alternatives to better my get-ready habits:

- Plan what to wear — from inside out and top to bottom — the night before.
- Give myself at least an extra fifteen minutes to put myself together in the morning (This means getting up an extra fifteen minutes earlier, unfortunately.)
- Make regular visits to the dry cleaners.
- Be very selective about the clothes I buy. Stop being impatient and buying "just anything."
- Think more about looking good.

Now, there's another aspect to the way we look that we simply have to face. Exercise.

I admire the people I see on the street with their little gym bags slung over their shoulders. They usually are in good physical shape, so I'm guessing they're coming or going to a gym. I have yet to join a gym or exercise club. It could be something I'll do when the mood hits, but at the moment I feel no compulsion to do so and there is no place in my weekly schedule to put gym time.

But I do exercise. By walking as much as possible, by tennis every other week, by dancing, and by doing a set of YWCA exercises fifteen minutes each night. This is not a program that would impress Arnold Schwarzenegger, but, for me, it's at least something.

And that's what we live-aloners have to do about exercise. Something. Anything.

Many of us get lazier as time marches on. This is a disaster. Your body will gradually get stiff as a board — or flabby as jello — and you won't look sophisticated at all.

Doing something physical with another person or with a group helps. A friend of mine wakes up at 5:30 in the morning and joins a group of people on East 40th Street. They go "race-walking" up First Avenue, past the United Nations building, up to the East 60's, then down Second Avenue to the East 40's again. These people, she tells me, swing their arms and walk very fast without breaking into a run.

When she told me of doing something so vigorous at that hour in the morning, my mind went at once to what I like to do at that hour — sleep. I knew I would never join that group, but my friend enjoys it and says she never felt better.

I go play tennis because I've made a date with a friend and I have to show up at the courts twice a month because we have reserved them. Knowing I'll see my pal and will have a good time spurs me on.

In Manhattan, because it is a small island with everything crammed together vertically, we climb stairs a lot: down to subways, up from subways, up and down stoops of buildings, up and down flights of stairs to go up to meeting rooms in hotels, upstairs to restaurants' restrooms.

We get a lot of stair exercise.

For five years I lived in a fifth floor walk-up apartment. That meant that once, twice, or three times a day I'd walk down and walk up five flights of stairs. Trips out of the apartment all had a definite purpose; I didn't saunter out for just anything.

(Even my garbage bag was given to the man I was currently dating. At the end of every date, I handed it to him to take down on his way out. He couldn't understand how I could end a romantic evening by handing him a bag of garbage. I told him I got tired of running down with it all the time, and he was really helping me out a lot. He didn't care. He simply didn't like kissing me goodnight over a bag of garbage. But, he took it down the stairs every time he came to call.)

When I left the walk-up and moved to an elevator building, I gained ten pounds in the first month.

Those stairs probably kept me and company who came to visit more fit than we'd ever been before or after. Stairs are great for grooming bodies.

So good grooming involves a lot of things — from the smallest details to the most daunting of physical activities. Since our egos, self-esteem, and self-image are at stake, carving out a daily niche for grooming is definitely worthwhile.

Good grooming makes us feel confident. And it prevents people from running in the other direction as we near them.

16 The Place Where You Live. Your Paradise

No matter where we live, small space or big space, simple or luxurious, it should be exactly as we want it. It's our retreat and it has to work for us.

When making a residence livable, don't skimp. This is not the time to pennypinch unnecessarily, because your place has to boost your morale, it has to comfort you, and it has to satisfy your soul as you come in from the outside world.

This isn't just "a place to live," it's a psychological haven. If your place isn't satisfying to you, you won't even be able to think straight, believe me.

If your place is giving you the blahs, think about redoing it in any scheme that suits your fancy: all-white, all-gray, all-red, all-yellow, high-tech, low-tech, or no-tech.

When I redecorate or fix up, I cut back for a few months on other things I've been spending on and, all in all, it works out semi-OK financially in the short run and very satisfying emotionally in the long run.

If you're living in a place that's too small, too noisy, or too crummy in any way, the easiest thing to do is nothing. The reason I know is because I've done it, nothing, while living in a place with problems.

I became immobilized.

The apartment I moved into in 1970 in New York City was small, but it was what I could afford at the time, and it was in a luxury high-rise and a well-kept building.

The New York City rental market in the mid-70's shot sky high, with very few affordable rentals available. We were frozen into living in our current apartments. So I stayed where I was although I longed to move a bigger place.

101

Then, in the late 70's, I began to get interference noise from neighbors who kept me awake at night. Noises and crashes jolted my sensibilities at every hour of the day and night.

I repeatedly went to the neighbors' door and pleaded with them to be quiet, but they refused to discuss it. I went to the superintendent and management company who said legally they could do nothing. It had to be settled by the two parties unless other people complained, too. Since my apartment was the only one abutting theirs, no one else heard the bangings and the crashings, so I was in a Catch 22.

I was going crazy with this living situation. I'd awaken bleary and red-eyed from being woken all night, I'd straggle in to work and wonder how I could solve the problem of living in a place that wasn't good for me — when there was no place I could afford to move.

This was the heights of the pits.

I'd even have taken a humble place that was quiet, over the luxury high-rise with inconsiderate neighbors.

I hated where I lived.

Several years later, two things happened. The first thing was that the disruptive neighbors moved away.

And the other thing was that I got myself *out* of my place by renting inexpensive summer houses just so I could have a change. I also started pet-sitting for our cat on the about the author page and several times moved myself lock, stock, and barrel into a friend's apartment (the cat's owner) while she was out of town for long periods of time. I lived in a wonderful, big, ultra-gorgeous apartment for months under this arrangement. It was a great experience.

This broke the chain of "Woe is me. Nothing will ever change about my living quarters."

For me, getting *out* of my apartment and onto new vistas, a summer house or living in a large glamorous apartment for half a year at a time, gave me a new outlook.

It made me want to fix up my small apartment in a way that suits me beautifully, which is the way it is now.

Living in a stagnant condition is horrible. But if you shake yourself up and say, "I want a great place to live in!" — it's a start. Don't kick yourself too hard if you're in a rut, just hard enough to get moving.

There's also the situation of living in a place that you know is temporary. Temporary is a magic word, as it can get us through almost any living condition. But, if they are not already so, we must always "warm up" temporary quarters before we inhabit them.

Once when I was in college I found room and board in exchange for babysitting.

The "board" was hot dogs a lot of nights of the week and old-fashioned Spartan food. It was not a wealthy family.

The room was literally nine feet by nine feet. In it were four things: a cot, a board that pulled down as a desk, a chair, and a glaring overhead light that made everything look like a jail cell.

This was the place I was to live in for the next year.

The first thing I did was go to good old Woolworth's and get one of their nifty pull-down shaded lamps that gave the room a warm glow. I put this over the dropboard that served as a desk. I bought two posters for the walls, some green plants, and a small carpet. In the glow of the yellow-shaded lamp, the place looked cozy. I was in business. In the room I could do the three things I had to do: study, eat, and sleep.

I don't recommend, however, making a home in a rabbit hutch forever. A cramped place is not conducive to expansive thinking.

But a one-person householder usually has a one-person income, and this sometimes intrudes on our lifestyles.

Here are the things to work on:

1. Fix up the place we're currently in.
2. Figure out how to get to the place of our dreams.

If you're living in a house or apartment that's not to your liking, simply regard it as a stepping stone to your next place. Make it liveable until you figure out how to move on.

Even if you have to take some money out of a savings account, get your place not only in shape, but ultra-pleasing to your eye.

I had the same furniture, carpets, and drapes in my apartment for a lot of years. (This is the same one I moved into in the 1970's.) I once liked my furnishings, but no longer.

I would walk slowly as I neared my place; I didn't want to go home. When I opened the front door and looked in, I'd sigh and feel a moroseness coming over me. I didn't know what was going on until a few months later. I was sitting in my living room looking around and said, "This place is as drab as the day is long."

I went into action. I decided I wanted the whole place done

over in cream, ivory, beige, and white tones. I've always wanted an "all-white" apartment. I don't know how I pulled it all together, but everything I did worked. Hallelujah.

I knew I couldn't spend tens of thousands on the project, but I did have to spend at least $1,500. I went to a discount carpet store and bought a luxurious new, thick, cream-colored carpet.

I gave away some awful armchairs, kept one ivory-colored one and bought several director's chairs in off-white fabric. I had new off-white venetian blinds installed; washed and bleached my sheer panel curtains for all the windows; and bought vanilla-colored towels and carpet for the bathroom and an ivory carpet for the kitchen.

I bought a vanilla-colored velvet comforter for my bed and paid a price I never thought I'd pay for any bedroom item. The comforter gives me such a feeling of luxury every time I look at it or lie on it, it was worth every penny.

I also purchased an ivory-and-gray striped sofa, but had a four-week wait until it was delivered. Every time I passed the store, I'd look at the floor sample, hold my breath, and wonder: Will it look good in my living room? Will the stripes jump out at me in my small place? Have I overdosed on cream and ivory colors?

When the big day came that the sofa was to be delivered, I was as antsy and excited as a child on Christmas morning. This was going to be the centerpiece of my whole scheme.

The men brought it into my apartment. The minute they set it down by the wall where it was to go, I could see that I picked the perfect couch — it was the right size, the right fabric, and the right look for my apartment.

The scheme of my theme worked. I felt like I had been plunked down in a vanilla ice cream vat — just what I wanted. What a difference this day was from the morose I-hate-this-apartment feeling of just a few months ago. (And I didn't break the bank to do it —just thought about it a lot and made *lists!* on a ruled pad ahead of time to save me from blundering. Forethought definitely helped.)

Now when I go home, I open the front door, put on a light, and feel wonderful that I'm there. I also have an "up" feeling when I'm there. The whole process changed my outlook.

I must say that in all the places in all the cities that I've lived in and fixed up, this one was touched with magic.

Fix up the place you come home to every day. This is the place you laugh in, cry in, entertain in, sit in, sleep in, and dream great ideas in. It's essential that it be your paradise.

17 What Are the Things You've Always Wanted to Do?

Before you can do the things you've always wanted to do, you have to figure out what those things are.

When I first lived alone, what I wanted to do was see parts of the U.S.

So for the first ten years, I moved to and lived and worked in four different cities — Los Angeles, two years; Honolulu, two years; San Francisco, five years; and back to my home, New York.

To move from one place to another had me in a state of constant activity:

1. Pack.
2. Leave an apartment.
3. Get on a plane.
4. Get off a plane.
5. Find a place to live.
6. Unpack.
7. Find a job.
8. Find friends.
9. Visit sights and surroundings of city.
10. Pack up again.

This didn't leave much time for boredom and inertia.

During those years, I also started reading self-help books to find out just what in heck I should do with my life and, here we go again, how to improve it. Underneath all the activity and reading, I had an inkling each city wasn't *exactly* where I wanted to live, so I always had a feeling "something" was going to happen to move me on. I never had a settled, quiet feeling.

When I came back to my home state of New York, I felt wonderful. I knew this was where I wanted to live, and I burrowed in.

I found the best job I'd ever had, met terrific people, found a good inexpensive apartment, and I felt like hugging the whole city of New York.

Contentment set in. But guess what.

I was bored.

I had nothing to do except work, have a social life, take vacations, and do volunteer jobs.

Something was missing and I didn't know what it was.

The answer was not in moving to another city. The answer was not found in any of my self-help books. The answer was not found in talking or thinking about the ennui that surrounded me. To this day I can feel the "deadness" of my life at that time — it was there no matter how much I listened to the radio, watched TV, or went out to dinners and parties and shows and plays.

A friend suggested I join him in taking adult evening classes. He'd been doing it for years and said he'd received a great education and had a good time in the classes.

I said: Ugh.

Doesn't the sound of "Adult Evening Classes" have a deadly ring to it? It did to me.

He brought me the catalog of one of the local schools, and I didn't look at it for weeks. When my boredom finally hit the highest level it could, I opened it up and flipped through it.

There were two things that interested me, a beginner's course in architecture and a beginner's course in writing. I thought as long as I'm always writing my ideas down on big pads of lined paper anyway, I might as well find out what this mystical thing called Writing is all about.

I signed up.

Life changed.

I'm not saying that someone signing up for a course will have his or her life's path altered forever because of it — but the course I signed up for was meant for me.

The first week we were assigned to write a story.

I wrote a story.

The second week of class mine was the first story to be read out loud in the class, with much praise from the instructor. She said it was the best story handed in, and told the class why. I thought my heart would pop out of my body.

In the next few weeks, the teacher told us all to go to variations: write poetry, start a play, write non-fiction.

We were having a garbage strike in New York City at the time. I had strong feelings about what was going on, and I wrote a play about strikes. A man in the class, a producer of off-Broadway plays, optioned the play.

I thought, *"What's* going on!?"

A year later my first play was produced off-off-Broadway, and since then thirteen more have been produced, the Corporation for Public Broadcasting bought some of them (including one called "The Ice Cubes," which brought in fan mail), and some of my plays have won competitions.

If there's a naggy thought in your brain, "Something's missing, something's missing," the thought isn't there by accident. It's God's way of knocking on your head and saying, "Let's get with it. Go out and get something out of life. Go out and put something back into life. Don't just sit there immobilized, feeling queasy, blah, and sorry for yourself."

I'm convinced that's what happened when the Evening Class catalog was plunked in my hands.

Even though living alone gives us the best chance we'll ever have to finally do EVERYTHING WE'VE EVER WANTED TO DO, it's not easy. We have to do a lot of experimenting to find out what it *is* we want to do, and we have to get rid of the inertia that keeps us locked up in our daily ruts.

You've got to mentally take yourself by the collar and shake yourself. It's the hardest thing in the world to do. But, like shaking out a carpet, the results are great.

Other people can tell you how you should be out doing things, but you're the only one who can get the show on the road.

You might also know what you want to do, but are afraid to make the leap. I've known people who wanted to go: into business for themselves; into show business; into selling real estate — all changing the course of their lives, but they didn't want to take the risks. A life without risks is nothing.

Security is, no question, a wonderful thing. I always feel that Gulliver in *Gulliver's Travels* had security in being tied down by all those strings the little people had pinned him down with. He was tied by others. We tie *ourselves* down by our own mental "Gulliver's strings" over ourselves.

If you don't go out and find out what your special talents are, you're depriving the world of something good.

There's a saying: "Many a flower is born to blush...unseen."

Get out of the house. Blush! Be seen!

Now, many people living alone have reached the point where they *don't* have the nagging feeling "something's missing." So if you're one of those, you're all set. Your life is filled to the brim, and we're all trying to catch up with you.

But for the rest of us who are always trying to fill up areas where we feel something is missing, we've got to do something.

There's a free catalog handed out in New York City that I glom onto every time a new issue comes out. There's always one or two things that I'd like to take. High schools, colleges, and Y's also have comprehensive catalogs. I'd suggest pulling them around your chair by a roaring fireside and reading them.

In some catalogs, I've seen the following courses. Most cost from $40 to $60 for four to six weeks, an hour or two every week:

How to Invest in Real Estate
Learn to Ballroom Dance in Six Hours
Introduction to the IBM PC
Understanding the Financial Pages
Learn to Type
Stop Procrastinating
Speech for Success
Assertiveness (Not Aggressiveness) Training
How to Make Money Catering
How to Land a Part in TV Commercials
Climb the Corporate Ladder of Success Easily
Start Your Own Business
The Visualization Technique: What Is It?
Surefire Methods to Improve Your Golf Game
Pick a Foreign Language and Learn to Speak It
Investing in Stocks, Bonds, and IRA's
How to Open a Travel Agency
Power Writing
Work and Sail Your Way Around the World
Horseback Riding
Tennis
Bicycle Riding for Beginners
How to Cook Like a Jewish Mother

Acting for Non-Actors
How to Read Music (Finally!)
An Introduction to Playing the Piano
Sailing for Beginners
Beginner's Writing Class
Letting Go and Moving On
How to Learn From Your Dreams
Learn How to Swim
How to Love Another Person and Make the Relationship
    Work

The list above is simply *classes* to enjoy or to learn from. Think of how many other things there are in the world to do: travel, teach, go on archaeological digs, volunteer to be a Big Brother or Big Sister, or be a Grandma or Grandpa to a child who doesn't have one, volunteer at a pet clinic, become a foster parent, change careers, learn house remodeling and repairs.

Let's go over what you have going for you with your current lifestyle.

You can do anything you want when you want to do it.

You have a lot of time to improve things in your own life which makes you better able to help others.

You have room to breathe — environmentally and psychologically.

You have energy because you're well-rested.

You can have noise when you want it, quiet when you want it. All musical and TV selections are yours.

You can light the place up when you want to, darken it when you want to.

You can have it as cold as you want it in the house, or as hot as you want it.

How many people would like to have these things? Plenty.

I have read about a formerly-married man and woman up in New England who have an unusual arrangement just to get what you have.

When they were married, they loved each other but simply couldn't get along. They tried everything not to get on each other's nerves, but it was pick, pick, pick, nag, nag, nag, and whatever else goes on in a marriage that isn't working. They are both professional people and have a lot going on in their lives, and did when they were married, too. Well, their life together was so contentious they got divorced. But they soon found out they missed each other. They started visiting each other, more and more; he driving over to her house, she to his. They would tell each other all their events of the day, and were the best of friends they always had been.

Now they struck on an idea. Why not buy one large house and DIVIDE it. They did just that. They bought a house, and she now lives on one side with a private entrance. He lives on the other side with his own entrance. They agreed to have a small door made between the two sides, just so they wouldn't have to go outside when it was raining when one of them visited the other.

They go for days without seeing each other. Then they call and make a date to get together. They're getting more accomplished now then ever before, they're both more fulfilled, and gone is the nitpicking (due to mutual confinement) that destroyed their marriage.

They haven't decided whether to get married again. They're simply living in this mode for the time being.

And here you are, having the flexibility, the space, and the time to live your life as you choose, without having to go through any big machinations to get there — you already are in an environment where you can be as creative, expansive, and productive as you see fit.

However, if you let a lot of ennui and grayness slip into your days, you'll be sunk. This is a two-sided affair for you. You have so much time to do everything you want to do. You have so much time, in fact, that, if you *don't* do things, the time will come crushing down and immobilize you.

If you become a hermit, do very little, and see only a few people, you're throwing away the best part of this lifestyle — the freedom to expand.

So start sweeping and stirring up what's hidden in the recesses of your mind and get busy. Don't just sit there. Live.

The most important thing in doing anything is having a *passion* about it — and then doing it.

I was passionate to get out of the empty feeling I had when I took my first writing course. I'm passionate in finding out about people and the comical things that happen in the world, and that's what I write about. I was passionate about getting my plays seen by people, so I stuffed envelopes with my scripts and licked stamps and sent them to theatres and producers until I was blue in the tongue.

A while ago I had a passion to finally learn to dance properly — after years of giving men black-and-blue toes from my klutziness and non-educated dancing feet. I didn't take myself to dance studios that charge thousands of dollars for a course. I instead took my recalcitrant feet to adult evening classes in ballroom dancing (foxtrot, swing, samba, mambo, etc.).

I always wanted to dance like Ginger Rogers, and although I'm still about 10,000 light years away, every class and every dance gets me a little bit closer. I go out dancing about twice a month now, and sometimes everything works right and my feet become Ginger Rogers's feet. What an experience.

I'm passionate about this book. I've turned the country upside down to find just the right publisher for it. It took me a year since I started writing it to find him.

I believe so much that living alone can be made into a good experience that I'll do everything I can to get the book into the hands of everyone who can get something out of it.

There were also lots of things I tackled *without* passion.

I've gone through the skiing experience, even lived and worked at Sun Valley, Idaho for a year. I was a lackluster skier, hated those bumpy snow mounds called "moguls," and many times couldn't wait till I got to the bottom of the hill so I could rest.

I also tried golf, and the first time I was on the golf course, I thought everything looked very outdoorsy and pleasant. When we got through with two holes, I said, "Are we almost done?" I was told a game is eighteen holes — sixteen more to go. My friends said the nineteenth hole was the clubhouse, the only vision that kept me going.

Other activities I've tried and felt a hundred percent lukewarm about are legendary.

I've seen scientists, psychologists, skiers, golfers, sports fans, poets, and singers with passion in their eyes — and I know they're on the right track. So am I, doing what I feel passionate about.

I'm sure there are things you've always wanted to do, but for some reason, didn't.

Nothing is too "dumb" to do. If you want to reach a goal, start at point one and do it.

Have you ever wanted to construct something? Have you ever wanted to go someplace unusual? Have you ever wanted to invent something? Write something? Paint something? Sculpt something? Fix something? Run for local office? Publish a newspaper?

Try out for the Roller Derby? Train to become a wrestler? Get that pad of lined paper out and put at the top: Things I've Always Wanted To Do.

You'll be surprised at what appears.

Now is the time for all good one-person householders to come to the aid of themselves and do what they've always wanted to do.

18 Social Events. Giving Them and Going to Them Successfully, Alone

We know what it's like to go to social functions with someone at your side. It's reassuring.

In the olden days, ten or fifteen years ago, some people wouldn't even invite someone who wasn't part of a couple to their parties.

Things are looking up as to how a "one-person" person is thought of now. We're not creatures from the Black Lagoon any more.

In fact, many times we're more interesting and fun to have around than someone who's one-half of a couple and who's locked into a dull marriage or relationship. These folks can be pretty sullen.

Social events are in two categories.

1. Those you give.
2. Those you go to.

I've been a liver-aloner for a while, and the parties and dinners put on in my house were always arranged and cooked by one person: me.

I've had every kind of get-together imaginable: opening night parties, a celebration of something successful happening to a friend, a celebration of anything — even a party to celebrate the end of winter.

I've given a few parties that were duds. Nothing worked right, conversation was stilted, and it was gruesome. I well remember and admire the honesty of one of my more outspoken friends who stood up at one of these fiascos and said, "This is an awful party and I'm going home." At least it made us all laugh, and we decided to throw in the towel and end the party. It just wasn't working.

Through trial and error I've finally learned how to give successful parties.

I put a lot of thought into them. I do all the ahead-of-time work and the clean-up work, and I've enjoyed some of my own parties more than many others I've gone to.

The biggest party I ever gave was for sixty-five people — they stretched from my outside hallway, through my apartment, and out onto the terrace.

My parties usually contain a mixture of ages — young, middle-aged, advanced age, any age.

There are only two prerequisites the guests must have: they must be interes*ted* and interest*ing.* They're dedicated to living a full life, they're not grumblers, they don't hog the time in conversations, they talk and listen with lots of interest and lots of humor.

No-humor, "down" people usually don't come to my parties. That's because invitations don't find their way to these people's mailboxes. If I've tried to help these people get "up" and failed, I leave them alone. A "down" person would definitely feel out of place at my soirees, and besides, I know they have soirees of their own. I've attended some of them.

I'm not going to give you every last detail of the A's to Z's of giving a party. I think we basically all know how to do it — find the occasion, get the inspiration to do it, make up a list of people to invite, phone or send out invitations, shop, cook, scrub, clean, get washed and dressed up a bit, and wait for the doorbell to ring.

I usually send out invitations a month ahead of time and ask for RSVP's. This will give you an idea of the size of your crowd at least, and whom to expect at the doorbell. There's one thing I've learned to do once the party starts. Stop being the host. I fix everyone a first drink (or have someone do it for me) and tell the person from that point on he or she may fix the drinks. I show the guests where the food is; I introduce whomever needs introducing. Then I just let it happen, and it usually does. There's a wonderful soaring of voices, chuckling, and laughter in short order. Most of the guests are doing something and are excited about their lives, and they're glad to spill the beans about their pet project of the moment — from giving up smoking to being called upon to redecorate the Taj Mahal. There's intensity and a festive feeling permeating the place. I'm right there partying with the rest of them, having a great time and forgetting that I'm the one who put on this shindig.

There's a focus, no matter how big or small, to the party. There's a *reason* I'm giving it, and I think this helps get rid of the "I wonder what I'm doing here" feeling we sometimes get at parties. When you come to a party at my place, you'll know why you're there — you're celebrating something that's happened, is happening, or is about to happen.

I don't take up guests' offers to help clean up when the party dwindles down. Why should they look into the mushy face of a piece of munched-on ham when they've been looking at and talking to interesting faces all evening?

I've gotten to the point where I enjoy the aftermath of a party. I survey the scene and bask in the glow of a good time.

I'll do only the major things of cleaning up — putting dishes in the kitchen sink, tossing out garbage, picking up only major pieces of debris, putting food away, getting chairs back to where they belong. The next day is time enough to do a session of dishwashing and complete straightening up. It's a good feeling to wake up the next day and see some of the remains of a successful party. You haven't wiped the whole place clean the night before, and there's the goings-on and high jinks that you can relive as you go about setting things in order.

By now, I can put on a party at a moment's notice. For one thing, I've served the same food, at small cost, for almost all the parties I've thrown and I don't have to give this aspect agonizing hours of thought and preparation time.

What is it? Picnic food. I figured everyone likes picnics, so why not serve these foods at every party I give? It cuts down on time and money spent, and it works out fine for me and my guests.

Here's what's on the tables: two platters of ham surrounded by Genoa salami, decorated with red cherry tomatoes and parsley sprigs; potato salad in a big wooden bowl; special bread, like French or whole grain where the seeds practically pop out at us; hot chili; cheese platters with every bit of cheese imaginable, the trays again decorated with cherry tomatoes and sprigs of parsley; a three-bean or mixed salad; and all other picnic food — pickles, mustard, potato chips, black olives, green olives, nuts, and nacho chips.

The bread's in big baskets, the tablecloth is a red checkered one, candles are glowing, and the drinks are flowing just right. How could you feel formal in a situation like this?

The whole food cost for the party comes to about $60, and the result is edibles that are substantial and that look and taste good.

Someday when I have more time and money, I'd like to vary my menu and have something other than the picnic food I've served so many times.

There are many types of food to serve, all you have to do is make the food something *you'd* like to have at a party.

I gave an impromptu celebration party a while ago and pulled it together literally in three hours. And it worked. People arrived, ate, drank, talked, laughed, and went home. I'm still getting thank you notes for "one of the best parties I've ever gone to." I'm so used to hearing how warm and wonderful my parties are by now, I can't imagine giving a phony-baloney party or one where people feel stiff and ill-at-ease.

Now. Going to social events is another situation. Being invited as one person, and actually walking through the front door into the social event as one person with no one dangling from any of our limbs takes some getting used to.

What will happen, as we improve our lives, our outlooks, our demeanor, our aliveness, is that people won't care that we're not part of a married couple and will throw caution to the winds and will invite us *by ourselves*.

This happened more and more to me as I became less and less bleak. At first, I was grateful that the people inviting me were overlooking the fact that I was just one. Now I take it for granted. It's normal that they invite me. I fit in and have a good time.

At the beginning of my live-alone life, I used to go to parties feeling out of place. I'd do artificial things, smile grotesquely, act shy, and mumble things that no one wanted to hear. Many backs were turned on me. I generally thought to die would be a good thing.

Then I found out some things that changed the course of my party life. First, I became more genuine and outgoing. Then I discovered that people want to talk about themselves more than anything else.

Since I'm naturally curious about why people do things and live their lives the way they do, it's the perfect way to get conversation started. How are you? What did you think of the weather (the game, the mayor's comments, the latest building that Donald

Trump put up) today?

The most important word to most people is *you.*

I once saw a cartoon where a famous author was talking at a cocktail party to a pretty young woman, and he must have remembered that the word "you" has to be put in the conversation every once in a while. So he leaned back, glass in hand, and said, "Enough about me and my book. Let's talk about you. What do YOU think about my book?"

I consider each person a Christmas present waiting to be opened. Sometimes when it's opened it's not what I wanted, but most times it's pretty interesting.

So instead of going to a party saying to myself, "What am I going to say?" I turn it around and say, "What am I going to ask?"

You'll be astounded at the bits of information, gems of wisdom, particles of dumb and egocentric mish-mash, and lessons in living that you'll get.

Talking to people and providing a good listening ear is almost like turning on TV: you'll get pap, information, education, or comedy. The person standing or sitting with you at a social event is giving these items to you uncut and unedited.

The last thing about a person alone at a party: don't talk *too* intensely with someone's spouse.

I've talked to the most dried-up, baldest, homeliest man in the room for a tad too long for his wife's liking. Lo and behold, she comes up to us, merely tolerates being introduced to me and says, "Hector, you must come with me and talk to Bill and Sally. They're talking about what you're interested in."

The wife thought I was going to steal Hector away from her. God love her.

When I become the other half of a couple someday, I'll probably do the same with my husband. And for now, as a one person, I accept an abrupt interruption of a conversation with the married man I've been talking with.

There's always another Christmas present waiting nearby for me to open.

What to Do With Those Wonderful Married People of the Opposite Sex. Should You Start with Them? Not Start with Them?

19

There are many times we meet fantastic people of the opposite sex, and some of them send our temperatures soaring.

Communication blossoms.

We eagerly start seeing them socially. We're happy. They're happy. They're terrific in all areas — looks, personality, lifestyle. They have absolute rapport with us, and we with them.

Some of these people, however, have one slight flaw.

They neglect to tell us they're married.

At some point we find out, inadvertently or advertently, that there are spouses, houses, kids, community property, pets, and summer homes in the picture, too.

This is no fun for us one-person householders to find out.

If we're dumb enough, we'll continue to see married people we've met under these circumstances. If we're smart enough, we'll drop the whole thing right there.

We're not only seeing married people, we're seeing mega-sneaky married people who deceive us from the outset by not telling us.

Sometimes people will tell us that they're married. But only after they know we're totally hooked. These people know when to spring the news: when we're blithering idiots and knocked out by our adoration for them.

They knew what they were doing, but we were flying blind and helpless. Now what?

There's also the category of *everyone* knowing about everyone's circumstances and letting the chips fall where they may. We go into it with eyes wide open. We know *full well*, from the first minute, that they're married, but we take the plunge.

The situations above have all the elements necessary to:

1. Totally grind down OUR egos and self-esteem.
2. Totally give the MARRIED people unbelievable boosts in ego, power, and control.

No matter if you're a man or a woman, it may be that a married person fits in with your psychological needs at the moment. So it goes.

Or let's say you're sitting there and feeling the need for something to add spice to your life.

At that precise moment, someone walks into your life and says you're delightful, smart, enormously good-looking, sensitive, caring, and all-around sensational.

You lap it up like a puppy gobbling kibble bits.

You're adored. There's no reason why you shouldn't be — this is one of the things the human ego strives for.

But in the case of the married adoring the non-married, it's coming from a wobbly foundation:

They gush over you.

You love it.

They leave.

You want more...

Unfortunately, there are built-in reasons for you to be a loser dating married people:

1. They'll charm you unbelievably while they're with you. Why shouldn't they? They don't go through much of life's crud with you — you see them mainly when everything's candlelit and artificially wonderful. They tell you great things about yourself. (You believe it, but why do they only want to see you once a week?) They go overboard about you, because what do they have to lose? There's no commitment.
2. After being with one of these charmers, it takes time to adjust to a "plain old-fashioned non-married person" who doesn't start off with a gush of sugar-coated compliments. (He or she's a little scared and nervous and is in the same boat as you are.) It may be like going from a Mercedes Benz to a Chevy, but let's say you're always borrowing the Mercedes, and the Chevy is *yours*.
3. You have to do a lot of waiting for the glorious times with the married person. It can't be when *you* want it. It has to fit in with his

or her schedule of spouse, house, kids, pets, summer house.

4. When they walk out of your door (where inevitably most of your get-togethers will be held — behind the door of YOUR place), they'll walk back into a household of bustling activity. You'll either go out to a bar and sit and stare at the bottles in front of the mirror, or else you'll sit in your one-person abode and stare at the telephone.

5. You're giving yourself a subconscious message that you're not good enough to get a whole person for yourself, so you'll take one that's already taken. Crumbs are all you deserve.

6. You don't spend Christmas, New Year's, Easter, Fourth of July, Labor Day, or Thanksgiving with these people. You'll rarely spend their birthdays with them. When something big happens in their lives, you're not allowed at the general celebration, but you and the person will simply have your two-person celebration. "It's all we need. It's better this way."

7. The unbelievable happy time spent with them cannot offset the harsh, "cut-off cold" feeling you have when they leave.

8. You're as disposable as a tissue, and your ego is as fragile as one. Yet you are the one who has to shoulder all the heaviness of the relationship.

9. He or she says he or she will soon divorce his or her spouse and marry you. He or she rarely does.

10. You won't be introduced to many of your co-conspirator's friends. You may do some things with your friends, but mainly it's the two of you, kid. There's no meeting of the important people in your married friend's life.

11. Whether you're a man or woman, you'll feel you're being used, not as a whole person, but as a plaything. You'll fight off these feelings. You'll say it doesn't matter, you're getting something out of it, too. When it continues that you're not able to call the shots, you'll start to feel you're in a losing proposition.

Here's what married people get out of this kind of arrangement:

EVERYTHING

There's nothing for them to lose, except the possibility of being found out, but that only adds glamor, suspense, and allure to the already interesting situation.

Here's a list of good things a married person adds to his or her life as a result of seeing you:

1. They're adored.

2. They're constantly being begged, "Please don't leave. I love you so much." What an ego-booster.

3. They have an interesting, fulfilled outside life. (They tell you they're only missing one thing: "A spouse who understands me." Believe me, their spouses understand them.)

4. You're only one of the diamonds on their big stringed bracelet. They allot you time like they do the other diamonds in their lives, but they make it quite clear not to become the Boss Diamond who has a say in anything.

5. You must fit into their schedule. The suspense of waiting for "the call" only heightens the actual meeting.

6. They have a warm bed to go home to after they leave you.

7. They have a feeling of security and control over themselves, their spouses, and unmarried people who are at their beck and call. Who could ask for anything more?

8. They have a delicious feeling of wrongdoing with what's going on, but they're getting away with it. What great fun.

Granted, it's exciting having a married person in your life. You may never get such compliments and hoopla again, and you may never again be with such a worldly, self-assured, slick person.

But, for me, it's a relief to let married people go and do their thing.

We all have phases in our lives when one thing or another seems right for us. At one point, smoking seemed right to me and I did it for many years and I thought I was getting fun and satisfaction from it. When I looked at it in the clear light of day, I said, "What am I *really* getting out of it?! A smelly house, a smelly me, and $1,500 paid out each year."

Goodbye, cigarettes.

Not an easy goodbye, but one that lasted.

There must be a Married Person's Manual that teaches all married people to say to single people, "My marriage isn't any good. We're just about separated. We'll probably split pretty soon. It's really dull. It doesn't work."

Bells should start ringing in our live-alone heads when we hear this kind of recitation. It's too cut and dried. Too pat. A real clinker of a cliche. Something's wrong with the picture.

I *finally* got this through my head when the last married person I ever saw went to Acalpulco, Mexico, with his wife. (Why do these almost-separated, almost-split people continue to go on exotic vacations with their spouses year after year?)

He came back, gloriously tanned and relaxed looking, and said they had a so-so time. Uh huh. . .

Then he handed me a small object wrapped tackily in some used gift wrapping. I opened it up and saw a hideous ring — an aqua blue lion's head with red stones as eyes. (Woolworth's could do better.) He said he bought it from a guy going up and down on the beach selling rings. I squinted my eyes. Thoughts were racing in my mind. All of a sudden it clicked. A ring from a beach vendor? And I've been sitting in the city for two weeks while he's gadding about? I've seen the light, at last. You're my last married person.

When my last married person walked out my door, I said to myself, "Why am I seeing someone who's going home to another person? Why aren't I seeing someone who's non-married and in the same world I'm in? With the same game plan? The same light at the end of the tunnel?"

Then I closed the chapter of seeing married people.

Not an easy goodbye, but one that lasted.

As one-person householders, the biggest thing we have is freedom. Including the freedom to tie ourselves up with married people.

Or, say "Thanks, but no thanks."

It's our choice.

Mingling with Couples, Families, and other People Not Living Alone

20

The Census Bureau says that the U.S. population as of September 1987 was 244 million.

If almost 22 million of us are one-person householders (nine percent), that leaves 222 million other people (ninety-one percent) who don't live the way we do.

Sooner or later, some of those 22 million people are going to ask us:

"How come you're living alone? Don't you want to get married?"

It's a natural question. After all, they see that the majority of people, including themselves, living as couples, families, or other groups.

Our households do not brim to the rafters with a group of anything.

When I first lived alone and was asked the questions, I'd sputter, hem, haw, and blurt out: "Well, um...er...gee, I don't know." I'd clutch my grocery bag containing cans of Soup for One and slink away.

It was a puzzlement.

I was happy living alone and I was pleased I wasn't in a bad or mediocre marriage. That much I was sure of.

I gave myself a project of coming up with an answer to settle it once and for all. I thought I'd try the old Tom Sawyer technique and have the questioner almost *envy* how I lived.

The questions: "How come you're living alone? Don't you want to get married?"

The answer: "I guess I've just been lucky! I'm aiming for a really great marriage. You know the kind?"

125

"I seem to be all right for now. Please bless my underwriters and my family, on an as-needed basis."

The person gulps, nods understandingly, and says, "Sure, sure, I know the kind. Hey, maybe you're doing the best thing after all."

End of discussion.

People are asking less and less as the live-alone group grows, as people are waiting longer to get married, and as the divorce rate remains at almost fifty percent of all marriages.

But it's always good to have an answer handy, so I recommend you experiment and come up with a good answer of your own:

Living alone suits me to a T.
It's the most luxurious way of living.
It's the lifestyle with the most freedom.
I'm very selective about whom I cohabitate with.
It's great to live alone.

You'll have your questioner's mouth watering.

Now comes the subject of mingling with the couples, families, and other groups not living alone.

When I first came back to New York, I started to re-acquaint myself with aunts, uncles, and cousins I hadn't seen for years. The cousins by this time had all married and were in cozy live-together units. In fact the whole family, East Coast, West Coast, and places in between, were coupled in one way or another. I was the first person in the family *ever* to live alone.

So there was a slight bit of culture shock and trepidation when we started mingling. I knew they were wondering what to *do* when ONE PERSON comes to visit?

As soon as they saw that I brought a little bit of fun and somewhat interesting conversations to the visit, they relaxed. Also, I didn't have two heads, webbed feet, and Godzilla scales sprouting from my ears.

They'd tell me things they'd been doing (pruning the trees, playing with the kids, fertilizing the lawn, making plans to build or buy a new house, winning sports or art competitions).

I'd tell them about my stuff (getting plays produced, working at a great company, giving a party for sixty-five people in a small apartment).

That party for sixty-five turned out to be one of the things that interested them the most. Sitting in their eleven room houses in the country, they couldn't imagine one person putting on a party for that number of people in a small city apartment.

They were beginning to see that my lifestyle had some interesting things going on in it, and they were generally warming towards me.

Over the next several years, they did a complete flip-flop in their opinions of my living-alone lifestyle. They saw that I could come and go and travel whenever and wherever I wanted to and was generally having a pretty good time.

In fact, one cousin said, "I can't imagine you doing anything you don't want to do. You have total freedom. What a life you've carved out for yourself!"

Although it's easy having a lot of friends who live alone because of the common ground we share, it's definitely a good idea to include as many of the other types of people as possible in our lives. It gives a balance that we need.

It's easy to be friends with couples. Usually you have something in common with the man or the woman, and the other accepts you and all of a sudden you're socializing with them.

Families are fun to visit — I like their big houses and all the nooks and crannies and interesting things to explore, experience, and reminisce about.

I like to see how people in couples or families or other groups live. They have fairly standard rituals — time to get up, time to get to bed, time to eat, who does what chore — and things work out.

It's a pleasure for me to spend time with these people and I genuinely look forward to my mingle time with them. So I go out of my door with anticipation, have a good time with them, and come back to my door with anticipation, refreshed and ready to get my one-person household humming again.

Thank you couples, families, and other groups for the pleasure of your company. You add a lot of joy to my life.

21   *Romances*

There is *nothing* like romance.

Romance was invented for a one-person household.

It's a great place to have one.

We can come and go to work every day, build bridges, turn the world upside down and make it notice us, but there's nothing like...romance.

A romance can usually cure what ails you.

If you're immobilized by inertia, all of a sudden you can be walking on air and jumping up lamp posts.

If you feel a sniffle or any other small illness coming on, it disappears quickly when there's a hint of romance in the air.

If you feel you look homely, somehow your self-image improves almost immediately. You become virile, radiant, beautiful, handsome, and an absolute knockout. All because you were told all this by the person you're having the romance with.

A romance can make life turn from dull black and white into full color.

If your house is untidy, it becomes clean. A romance demands a good stage.

If your hair and toenails are in shabby condition, suddenly you find the impetus to make them slick and shiny.

If your underwear is raggedy, you dash out to the store and buy jazzy understuff.

There are five stages a romance can go through:

1. You meet.
2. You get along famously.
3. You stay with each other.
4. You don't get along famously.
5. You part company.

The twosome of you comes out either as a full-blown adult relationship, or it doesn't. Romance sends us pretty direct messages.

As a start, let's say you're one person living in your one-person household, going out of the house doing fairly interesting and productive things, coming home, going out again.

Then a person appears out of nowhere and looks at you in a different way than other people look at you. They're interested in you and you like it that they're interested in you.

Without many words being spoken, the vibrations begin, and both of you are aware of the feelings going on.

Then it proceeds.

The ever-present butterflies are doing their thing in your individual stomachs.

You stare at each other.

You can't believe the person adores you as much as you adore him or her.

Time seems eternally long when you don't see the person.

The times you spend with each other are unbelievably warm and fantastic.

I can't think of a more delicious setup than this. Everything works, and we feel we're the human being we were meant to be. We're at the top of the world. It's perfect.

Every love song makes sense. The people who wrote them knew what it was all about.

Many things that happen in a romance are universal, but there are some things a one-person householder has that other people living in groups don't have:

1. You have time to prepare yourself for the meeting with the adored one.
2. You have the privacy of your own place in which to conduct the romance.
3. You can spend all your energy on the person.
4. You don't have to let anyone in the outside world know what's going on until you're ready to talk about it.
5. You can use your place for doing *anything* you want to with your adored one — at any time of the day or night.

Let's say the romance has developed and grown naturally, and you're both thrilled about the whole thing.

"We're both strategically driven,
so we're not ruling out the possibility of that
igniting into love."

You've gone past "Go" and are ready for the next segment, "reality." If certain realities are acceptable to the two of you, the romance will continue. But if living in the real world with your honey-bunny makes you uncomfortable, this is not the person for you.

Here are examples of the real world:

1. Helping each other out of financial crises.
2. Working on an intricate project together.
3. Helping each other through soggy illnesses or waiting for each other after a grueling session at the dentist.
4. Being with each other when one of you is in a grouchy mood.
5. Seeing each other after work, non-glamorous and tired.
6. Getting lost, having a breakdown, or going through any emergency in a car, on an expressway, late at night, with no phone in sight, *and* in a rainy downpour.

Going through some of the above will tell you how strong the bond is between you.

On another topic, one of the temptations of living alone and going through a hot and heavy romance is to stop seeing or communicating with all your other friends and contacts.

You'll think, "I've got everything I could ever want with my adored Sweetie, why should I bother to call or see Jane, or Harry, or Aunt Minnie?"

This is not a considerate thing to do, first of all. Secondly, it's not to your advantage. No matter if the romance goes on or stops, you'll want the support of Jane, Harry, and Aunt Minnie.

So continue to be a nice guy and don't ignore them while the romance is rolling along its jolly way.

You can even take your poopsie-woopsie and *visit* Aunt Minnie. At least you'll have something different to talk about — other than yourselves and your romance — when you leave Aunt Minnie's. You can talk about her.

Go out to dinner with Jane. Bring another person along and make it a foursome. Maybe the other person and Jane will hit it off, and you'll again have something fresh to discuss.

Visit Harry and find out his news. Maybe he's starting a new business and you could give him some encouragement. Maybe he's going to Bangkok and won't be seeing you for a while. Maybe he's found a romance of his own and wants to tell you about it.

One more thing. In the midst of your romance, answer your phone once in a while. If you have an answering machine, don't let your friends talk to the mechanical message, day after day, week after week. *Talk* to people who phone you. They'd like to hear your voice to know you haven't died in the middle of your romance.

If by chance the romance doesn't work out, it's not fun, but it must be ended. If a relationship is ready to be terminated, cut it right there.

It's easy to fall into the trap of dragging it on for years, because for a one-person householder *any* relationship fills a void. But you're wasting your time and your life by continuing with a person who's not for you.

If only one of you wants to break up, things can get a bit messy.

Even if the romance ends in a civilized way, there's a feeling of loss. You have to fill up the emptiness with things that make you feel good.

Doing the old embryo routine and hiding under the covers is a popular remedy. Other remedies include taking a trip, going out dancing, crying in your beer, or visiting your mother and asking her to fix you some chicken soup.

If all goes well with your romance, however, you probably have the makings of a two-person household coming up.

Congratulations. Do it!

And give thanks to your one-person household that served as a heaven and a haven for the fledgling romance, breathed life into it, and made it flourish.

22 *No Romances*

If you're in the mood for romance, but nothing is perking, you might want to plan a course of action.

This doesn't mean that if you're a woman you have to fly to Arizona or Alaska because the statistics tell us "This is where the men are." Or, if you're a man, to fling yourself on an ocean cruise because "That's where the women are."

There are plenty of men and women in your own area, and you'll find them mainly by going out and doing what *interests* you.

Going somewhere out of your way to find romance is artificial. What if you don't like Arizona or Alaska? Why go there and sift through their populations looking for Mr. Right? You don't like boats or the ocean, you get seasick, and your heart's not into socializing on the high seas. So why go on the cruise?

More matches have been made in heaven by people who met mountain climbing, horseback riding, at seminars, concerts, tennis courts, ski slopes, conventions, and other places where people go out of interest.

When I started to take dancing lessons, and then went *out* and danced, whew! what chances for romances I had. I was startled to find out how many men in the world are looking for Ms. Right. My ego got a much-needed shot in the arm, too, as I was being swirled around the dance floor being told sweet nothings.

When I go out dancing with friends, my thoughts are how to learn to dance better, have a good time, get exercise, and be with the opposite sex.

When I finally find someone I want to romance me and vice versa, it will be a welcome bonus.

If you're not finding romance on any menu, then for Pete's sake, at least *flirt.* You're going to lose all identity with your gender if you don't use your God-given right to bat your eyelashes or smile seductively at someone.

Have you ever seen a picture of a gnarled hermit wandering around his hut in the wilds? This person has an expressionless face. There's no vigor or verve showing in any part of the hermit's body. He hasn't had a romance in years, and it shows.

I'm not saying we'll be like this person if we don't have romance in our lives. What I am saying is: lack of romance dries us up — physically and emotionally.

Then there are the times when we're simply not in the mood for a romantic happening. Who knows why. Maybe we're busy on a project, maybe we've just gotten over a relationship that didn't work, maybe it feels good to be unencumbered at the moment. (A romance does take a lot of time, concentration, and physical stamina.)

This is OK, but we must not get "dead" in this area.

A friend of mine who had been romance-less for a few years told me a handsome, swarthy, green-eyed dry-cleaner was driving her nuts. She'd look at him and mentally melt. She said, "I won't pursue him, he's married, but it's nice to know that the sap can still rise." She compared herself to a maple tree that still functioned.

If the sap doesn't rise, what you have is a dried up, not very juicy maple tree.

When you don't have romance in your life, you're not getting any cuddling, billing, cooing, tickling, or nibbling on your ears and other places. You're missing something in the sex department. Read Dr. Ruth for suggestions in this department. She'll give you reams of advice.

If you're without a romance, don't hit yourself over the head about it. But do keep yourself spruced up so you'll be in good shape when the right thing comes along, and keep going to those places and doing those things that interest you.

You'll notice this chapter is shorter than the one on romance. That's because No Romance isn't as interesting as Romance.

Enough said. Romance is out there — probably in a place you'd least expect to find it.

23 *What to Do When the Blahs Hit*

This is the toughest subject of all.

When the blahs hit a one-person householder, it's gruesome.

I'm sure it could be the same for someone living as a couple, in a group, or any other way, but the only way I know about the blahs is from having them while living alone.

When I was a child and lived with my family, I found out two ways to ease the blahs:

1. Stick out my tongue.
2. Go into a corner and not talk to anyone.

As an adult, I grappled with several solutions. Here they are, from least effective to most:

1. Make believe the blahs aren't happening. Keep a stiff upper lip and feel miserable.
2. Know that the blahs have arrived, and knock myself over the head and blame myself for them, thereby making the situation worse.
3. Think that everyone has a wonderful life — except me. Everyone has a great job, a beautiful house, terrific children, sailboats, fabulous people they're married to. It's only me who has the dregs.
4. Do nothing. I say to myself, "This is the way it is. My life's blah and I'm a dud." I let the blahs take over, and I live with them.
5. Sit down, lie down, or fall down and have a good cry. I can't recommend this solution more highly. It solves *so much.* It's got to be a real good ranting and raving and moaning into the pillow, bedspread, or sofa to make a good cry work to your advantage. Pull

out all the stops, think how miserable everything is, and just let go. When the crying stops, you'll think to yourself, "Things really couldn't be *that* bad, could they?" The answer is usually that most parts of your life are really OK after all, and you feel better. Crying is one of the most normal things a person can do. It wasn't given to us for no reason — it was given to us so we could uncork our emotions once in a while.

6. The ultimate and best solution to solving the blahs, however, is to take action and do something or go anywhere — even to the Korean grocer to get a bunch of carrots or the Post Office for stamps. At least you're functioning. Maybe this will un-blah you enough to phone up a kind person and ask him or her to meet you for a cup, glass, or bite of something fortifying.

Sometimes when I'm immersed in the blahs, I say over and over to myself, "Do I ever feel negative. I really feel down." Then I'll answer, "Well, it's no wonder. You've had a lot of negative and down things happen lately. You're only reacting like a normal human being. Negative things make people feel negative."

Then I feel a little better. At least I've explained to myself why I have the blahs.

I'm an expert at the blahs, I've had them hit me so many times. But I think it goes with the territory. When we don't have built-in people living with us, we're not being given any stimulation by any-one — and a dormant environment is the best breeding ground for the blahs.

This is what *not* to do when you get an attack of dreary blahs:

1. Think it's *all* the fault of other people.
2. Think it's *all* your fault.
3. Phone people up, tell them about your blahs from A to Z and in great detail. People generally don't like hour after hour of moaning and groaning. So don't be surprised when they say after a while that they've "got to go now. Something is: burning on the stove, falling off the roof, knocking at the door, or making growling noises under the bed." Click!
4. Get grouchy and mean and take it out on other people.
5. Turn into a sourpuss.
6. Pout and get snippy.

If you feel any of the above coming on, crawl under the bed covers and don't try to solve anything at the moment. Have a radio next to the bed and listen to *anything*. Find a talk show where people are calling in with their problems. Listen to classical music, pop, rock, country and western, or golden oldies of the 20's, 30's, 40's, 50's, 60's, or 70's. Let only the music go through your head and let yourself drift in and out of snoozing.

When you get up, you still may have the blahs, but at least you'll be rested enough to deal with them.

There's also something that can be done in the midst of your blahs or blues that can be very productive.

Don't reject this idea out before at least mulling it over. It really can work.

Think of someone you know who owns a video recording camera and have that person make a ten minute tape of you. Just you.

If you don't know anyone who has a video camera, go to a professional studio and pay to get a video of yourself.

When you see how you come across as you watch the tape, you'll be amazed.

I'll tell you why.

We might have images in our heads that were left there by a few semi-unfriendly people in the past; images that we aren't quite up to snuff. For whatever reason, these people from our past enjoyed putting us down. OK.

You might have one picture of yourself in your head, but the picture that comes out through a video camera is the *actual* you. And it's probably better than you thought. I'd say almost unqualifiedly that you're going to be pleasantly surprised when you first see yourself in action on the screen.

Do the taping informally. Have the person who is doing the taping prepare a few questions to ask you. About any topic. When you start speaking, you can't help but be your real self, because there's no pressure involved. Just a give and take of questions and answers going on.

OK. The tape is immediately played back to you on an adjoining VCR, or else you take it to a VCR somewhere and have it played.

You look at the screen where you appear.

You don't look like a "poor soul" at all. Everything about you is working. Your eyes light up when you feel thoughts and express them verbally. You look calmer, more in control, more together, more like a human being ... a better you than you ever saw in your mind's eye.

When I decided to do this, just recently, I called an actress friend of mine who teaches a class called "Get Yourself Camera Ready," a course for actors studying to do TV commercials.

I sat in front of the camera (which doesn't make any noise ... so you don't even know you're being recorded), and my friend gently asked me questions about the topic of living alone successfully. We had a great time.

But the best part was when I took the tape home and played it on my recently-bought VCR. I was astounded. This was the first time I'd ever seen myself on film, and I looked like a fairly decent human being.

If you have a tape of yourself made, you'll see that there are more handsome and charming parts about yourself than you ever imagined. It took a video tape to give me a correct image of myself. I'm OK and a fairly nifty person.

The procedure is one that will definitely uplift you.

The blahs should be looked at as messages: "Something's not going right in my life, and I'm unhappy." Does something need to be added, altered, or done away with in your life? Is there anything you could do differently that would help? Are there things you can change? Those are the ones to work on. Are there things you can't change? Acknowledge them and don't try to change them.

It could be any one of a number of things that you can fix up: your job, your social life, your relations with relations, your money intake, your self-image.

If something in your life isn't working, use the messages the blahs are giving you. The blahs could turn out to be your best friend. They're telling you to pick yourself up, dust yourself off, and repair things in your life.

So it goes with the blahs. The more they help to get things fixed up in my life, the less I'll need them.

24
What to Do About the Five-Week Holiday Season — Thanksgiving to New Year's

For the person living alone, the five-week holiday season at the end of the year isn't the easiest nut to crack. First of all, we've got to get ourselves half-decent to get invited anywhere. Then, we don't want to go and be with people who are downers and pull us under when we're trying to get a little bit up on the ladder. We want — as everyone does — to have the holidays up, but we don't want to become a frantic wreck from the strain. Many families have certain rituals built around the five-week holiday period from Thanksgiving to New Year's, and they basically do the same thing year after year and they find this very pleasurable.

Then there are some of us who don't have set rituals, and each holiday season brings new sets of circumstances.

I now know how to get the most out of the holidays, but it took me a while to learn some things.

Holidays are rich with meaning, and we should treat them with the attention they deserve. If you slough off holidays and say that you don't care what you do when they arrive, things aren't going to turn out well. You'll have a nagging feeling that something isn't right in life. And something isn't right. You've just dropped yourself out of "people" traditions, whether Thanksgiving, Hanukkah, or Christmas, that have taken a few years or a few centuries to develop.

There's a reason for these traditions, and we're missing the boat if we don't join in.

There are dumb ways to go through the holidays, and there are good ways.

Here are some things I advise you not to do:

1. Don't spend any of the important days doing anything you resent or don't like to do. I remember spending a Christmas or two with a lot of negative Nellies and Neds. They'd complain about every-thing under the sun, and I'd say to myself, "This is Christmas!?" Don't spend a holiday with any group not to your liking, just to be "with others." This is pits, not pizzazz.

2. Don't spend a holiday feeling sorry for yourself. It immobilizes you and you end up doing nothing.

3. Don't go *anywhere* you really don't want to go, but "should" go to. This is disaster of the first order. The look on your face will tell all. And you'll feel worse at the end of the day than when you started out. You didn't do what felt natural.

4. Don't end up by doing absolutely *nothing* except starting at the wall or at the television set. One year when little else seemed appealing to me on a Thanksgiving, I continued writing a play I was working on. I had a few calls from people wishing me Happy Thanksgiving, and asking what I was doing. When I said I was working on a play, it seemed a tad odd — both to them and to me. But it was what I wanted to do over the other choices I had, and for that Thanksgiving it felt right. I ate a TV turkey dinner that night, said my thanks, and it ended up that the play eventually won a national competition and had a good production in Boston. So instead of doing nothing on a holiday when your mailbox isn't loaded with invitations you want, or you don't want to create a get-together of your own, go into an expansive, creative mode that's to your liking. It's an experience.

5. Don't let holiday hysteria hit you between the eyes. Stay calm. Don't get frantic.

6. Stay off crowded buses if at all possible, especially as a holiday comes closer. The rains get heavier, the umbrellas get sharper, and the shopping bags and boxes bigger. A holiday season is not when you want to get hit in the eye by people who are not calm.

Here are some things I recommend doing on the year-end major holidays:

1. Accept any invitation from relatives who are fun and visit them for a day. You and they will feel good to see each other's faces.

2. Take a trip to Bermuda or some exotic place with a favorite friend.

3. Make a get-together at your place. As a one-person householder,

you do have a *household* — and you can make things happen at that cozy warm place, instead of waiting for things to happen outside.
4. Accept an invitation at a close friend's place where you really want to be.
5. Decorate your front door with the spirit of the season — it *gets* you in the spirit of things.
6. Put a pumpkin on the table at Thanksgiving, for heaven's sake, any kind of tree up at Christmas, and some festive glasses out on New Year's Eve or New Year's Day and invite a pal over for an hour or two.
7. Do something good for someone else.

Item 7 above is an interesting one and is worth looking into. There are many people who help out the needy in a way that suits both themselves and the people they're helping.

I read about a man in New York City who most every Christmas does this: he buys $20,000 (Twenty Thousand Dollars) worth of gloves of all sizes every year. Then, on Christmas Day, he walks around the city and gives a pair of gloves to *anyone* whose hands are cold.

He doesn't lecture anyone; he doesn't ask anything of the recipients. All he's looking for is to make cold hands warm, no matter whose hands they are: students, Bowery residents, middle-class people. No questions asked.

His gesture started by his memories of walking around the city with his father in the bitter winter, and he remembered the cold, bare hands of so many who simply didn't have gloves.

He has to be a fairly affluent man — $20,000 isn't a mere bag of shells. But it's his way of adding to the warmth of humanity.

There are plenty of places and people who can use us during the holidays and the rest of the year for what we can offer — even just showing up and talking to someone.

If you have a regular ritual about the major days of the holidays at the end of the year, all the better.

Through lots of experimentation, I've found that, for the time being, I like spending Thanksgiving with relatives, Christmas giving a party at my house, and New Year's Eve at Times Square.

I'm sure the way I spend the holidays will change as time goes on, and I'll continue to experiment on how a one-person householder can get a lot out of them.

One thing for sure, I'm enjoying them more and more — the more *I* put into them.

25 Your Birthday. Once More with Feeling

If we've lived a certain number of years, we're a certain number of years old.

There's a new sweatshirt out with the saying on it, "Improved with Age." I'm going to buy it.

If cheese and wine don't hide the number of years they've improved, I can't see why people hide their number of years.

It's a real trip — and an interesting one — to go upwards in age. Since we don't have any choice in the matter, why not enjoy it?

I must bring up one important person in this discussion: no matter what your age, to George Burns you're a mere child. At this writing, he's ninety-two.

This man's got it figured out: live, live, LIVE!, till your nineties, till you're a hundred, and more.

Burns has a contract with the Palladium Theatre in London that he play a two week engagement on his hundredth birthday.

He doesn't care that he'll be a hundred years old. He cares that he got a TWO WEEK ENGAGEMENT AT THE PALLADIUM!

I mean, that's enthusiasm.

And he has enthusiasm about his days — writing his book about what he does to stay fit at eighty and ninety, doing movies, doing commercials.

And he doesn't conceal his age. Neither should we.

What's the big deal?

Employers pretty much know how old we are, people with whom we socialize have a pretty good idea, so why keep the number of years we've lived hidden under a tight lid?

To me, age has always been a very thought-provoking thing. When I was seven I thought, "This is interesting, this is what it feels like to be seven. I wonder what it will feel like to be twenty-seven, fifty-seven."

I remember walking down the street with a friend when I was about to have my forty-seventh birthday. And I said, "Just think, in three years I'll be fifty! Isn't that great? I wonder what fifty will feel like?"

She said most people wouldn't think getting older was great. I said, "I really like the number of years I've lived."

And I still do.

Each year has been filled with situations that are new, interesting, challenging.

So why wipe out the years?

I've lived fifty-four years, and so has Sophia Loren, Brigitte Bardot, and Gloria Steinem, and none of us hide how many years we've lived.

When the subject of age comes up, smile, with every character line on your face gleaming, and say your age with a lot of pride. Being coquettish and furtive about one's age is passe.

I have a theory that the people who either hide their age or lie about it age faster than those who bring it out into the open. And people who do mention their ages look younger than they are. I think hiding one's age puts a strain on people.

There is something that should be brought up about one-person householders having birthdays: how to spend a birthday.

No matter what you do on the day of your birthday, you must do something. I don't think anyone can feel much lonelier than having nothing planned for the day, not acknowledging it, and spending it with no one. This can make one feel lower than the bottom of an alligator's belly.

I experienced that several birthdays ago, and I never want to have it happen again. I don't ever remember a more pathetic day.

Somehow, in past birthdays, things seemed to automatically work out — either people gave me a small party, or I'd be taken out to a special expensive restaurant by my current flame the night of my birthday, or someone would take me to a show, or I'd simply arrange to meet someone for dinner. My birthday would be a big or little celebration, but at least *something* occurred.

When my bottom-of-the-barrel birthday occurred, I was completely surprised by its being so ghastly. For some reason that year I didn't mention to many people that my birthday was coming up.

A few cards came in from out-of-town friends and relatives before the Sunday of the birthday, and that was fine. I thought everything was O.K.

The days came and went before the birthday, and still nothing was coming up as to what I'd be doing that was special. I shrugged it off and thought something was bound to come up.

I had a two-hour workshop with a writer friend planned for early Sunday afternoon, and naturally assumed I'd get some kind of invitation from somewhere to do something in the evening, just as on other birthdays.

Thursday came, Friday came, and I wasn't being deluged with invitations to do *anything*, I thought something would break at the last minute. Saturday came, still nothing. I became immobilized. I was embarrassed. I was mortified. I wasn't going to be doing anything on my birthday.

Sunday morning came, and it was the first time in a long time that not even a relative called. I was in a funk. Not only weren't friends rallying around, my immediate family had decided this was the year not to call me and wish me "Happy Birthday."

I dragged myself to my friend's house to have our writers' workshop, and she wished me a Happy Birthday when I came in. I thought, well that's good, at least I get one Happy Birthday.

At the end of our two hours of working on our writing projects, she brought out a little cupcake with a candle on it and gave me a card. That cupcake and card meant more to me than anything I could think of. At least a tiny little fete had come about. I told her I was thrilled, and I was. Internally I was thinking, what if we hadn't arranged to have the writers' workshop this day. I wouldn't even have gotten the cupcake.

I schlumped back home, and came face to face with the fact that this was the oddest and most pathetic birthday I'd ever had.

Of course, there may be people who are perfectly happy and well-adjusted. They have everything in life they want, and simply *don't want* to celebrate their birthdays or have any fuss made over it for whatever reason. They have convinced us they don't want to celebrate their birthday, and that's that. I'd take their word for it and let the whole thing drop.

I think most of us like to have some kind of a fuss made over us on our day. After all, it's the one day in the year that's all ours. It's not any kind of a special religious holiday or national holiday, it's a day that belongs especially to us.

I'm not saying we have to hire a brass band and rent a banquet hall each year. But in all likelihood, some small celebration can be whipped up.

If you're living near your family, they usually will come through for their favorite nephew, niece, son, daughter, cousin, aunt, uncle, or whomever you are. You don't even have to think about it. Some things happen automatically.

I had done everything wrong. I soon pieced the puzzle together and came up with the things a one-person householder should *not* do prior to his or her birthday:

1. Don't tell anyone it's coming up.
2. Sit and wait for people to tell you what they have planned for you. Even wait until the day before your birthday. You're sure someone's going to come through.
3. Don't make any plan of your own.
4. Get bluer and bluer as the day arrives.
5. Do absolutely nothing special on the day of your birthday.

I have a friend who never mentions his birthday until a few weeks after it's passed. I'm always sorry that I missed it and didn't even send a card. But because it's over with for the year, I fail to write down the date — and this has gone on for years. When I ask what he did for his birthday, it's usually been, "Nothing really came up, so I didn't do anything."

Now I can see why nothing came up. The birthday was ignored, not mentioned, and buried by him. My friend said that he didn't do this intentionally, he usually wished something would happen, but it didn't.

Well, I'm here to tell you that I think something should take place on the birthday of the one-person householder. If we don't even want to acknowledge the fact that we were born and make a little to-do about it, self esteem is not rampant.

If nothing is happening automatically, "make" something happen. I know now that there were several things I could have done to prevent my disaster a few years ago:

1. TELL people my birthday was coming up.
2. TELL people I hope to do something special. If nothing special seems to be coming up...

3. Then I can make something special happen.
4. Ask a friend to go out to dinner.
5. Make a celebration at my own place. Combine it with other things that I or friends are celebrating at the moment.

Item 5 is what I did this year. I threw a lot of celebrations in on the day of my birthday: someone getting a new job, someone getting a book published, someone quitting smoking, someone going on a trip to China, and me, someone having a birthday. It was one of the best birthdays I've ever had.

I'll never let a birthday of mine fall through the cracks again.

It can either be one of the best days of the year, or the worst. And I'll take the former.

Whenever any of you one-person householders, has a birthday, give yourself a big "Happy Birthday" from me. I'm voting for you.

26 Vacations. Call the Airline, Pack a Bag, Turn Off the Lights, Close the Front Door, and Go

You live alone.

You want to go on a trip.

You pick a place.

You go.

You have unbelievable freedom to go when, where, and how you like, and everything is out there waiting for you.

I strongly encourage you to pick yourself up, dust yourself off, pack a small bag, get out of the house, and *travel.*

I know there are people who simply don't like a change in routine, and these people are not meant for traveling. They like everything in its place and no surprises. That's OK. Some people prefer their living rooms and easy chairs more than anything else, and there's nothing wrong with that.

But for the rest of us, the most eventful things can happen to us when we travel, whether we travel by ourselves, with another person, or with a group.

From my point of view, one of the best ways to travel is solo. Why? Because you're free to:

1. Pick your destination.
2. Decide what to do once you're there.
3. Investigate anything you want...down any alleyways and crooked streets that look intriguing.
4. Meet as many people as you want. You'l be surprised at how easy it is.
5. Sleep as late or early as you want.
6. Let surprises and unexpected things happen as they may.

There's a good chance that you'll have the time of your life traveling alone. Serendipity seems to happen around every corner to the solo traveler.

Traveling with other people is fun, too. I've enjoyed taking major trips with others — with friends to the Rockies, to Reno, to Lake Tahoe, to Ensenada, Mexico, to historic Coronado Island off San Diego, and on ski trips to Vancouver, B.C., and with romances to even more romantic places — Bermuda, Montreal, Copenhagen, London, the Caribbean Islands.

When we travel with someone else, we have something in common to share, and it's fun to reminisce about the trip later.

(It also lets us find out a lot about each other. I say there are three ways people can find out if they're compatible: when they live together, work together, or *travel* together.)

Back to a trip by yourself. It can be the most liberating thing you've ever done.

If you don't look or act like Jack or Jacqueline the Ripper, or aren't strange in a major way, you've got a very good chance of having a good time.

Let's look at Why, How, When, and Where all this traveling-alone stuff happens.

WHY

Other than that it's fun, there are generally two reasons why people travel alone:
1. Other people whom you'd like to have join you aren't free at the same time you are.
2. No one you know wants to go where you're planning to go.

HOW

There are two basic ways to travel on your own:
1. Being on your own from beginning to end.
2. Signing up with a group.

You'll notice that I didn't say "Tour Group," although that's what most traveling groups are called. If you have reservations about "Tour Groups," I understand your feelings.

When people used to mention "Tour Groups" to me, I'd either mentally hold my nose or tilt it haughtily in the air.

The name had a bad connotation. It seemed to mean you had to schlep around cathedrals and museums with a bunch of uncultured, loud, uncouth Americans in Hawaiian shirts and straw hats, and all the locals would point at you and snicker.

That was my impression until I decided, in 1969, that I wanted to see Russia. I found out one doesn't just knock on Russia's door and they'll let you in. You have to be guided by Intourist once you're over there, and the main method of travel is with an organized tour.

"An organized tour," I sniffed. "How gross."

But my desire to see Russia took over. If I had to go with a tour group, I'd go with a tour group.

I signed up, thinking I didn't have to lock myself in with these people, I'm used to traveling alone, I'll only be with them for the absolute minimum that's required, and I'll strike off on my own for the most part.

We had ninety people in our group, and to my surprise, most were intelligent, humorous, curious, and interesting.

Many were in couples, and about ten of us were singles, including a tall, good-looking blond man (my favorite kind) who, I found out, was taking the trip on the same basis I was: "I'll be with the group if this is the only way I can see Russia, but I'm not into the group mentality."

Well, the trip totally blew the lid off my thinking about traveling with a tour. We had things prearranged for us, banquets, dances, nightclubs, meals, visits to places one could never have arranged without some good coordination.

I was perfectly free to split away from the group whenever and wherever I desired, as long as I met up with them to board a plane to go to another city.

I did see a lot of sights with the group, but also roamed around on my own, heading off in any direction to see where it would take me. I met a lot of Soviet people on my own, simply on the street, or standing in line to buy ice cream, or sitting on a park bench.

Since I like one-to-one contact with people when I'm visiting in a country, my strolls paid off. I had a Berlitz phrase book with me — English to Russian, Russian to English — and I got along famously. I even ended up putting together a party in my hotel room with some Russian theatre folks I met.

The flexibility also allowed a romance to develop, slowly but surely, between me and the tall, good-looking blond man who liked his independence as much as I did.

In fact, we liked independence so much, we started doing a lot of it together.

By the time we were in the last city on the tour, Leningrad, we were spending almost all of our time by ourselves.

Group? What group. Are we with a group?

When we joined the other eighty-eight people for a meal, we realized we had eighty-eight pairs of eyes, or *176 total eyes* watching us. A storybook romance was unfolding right before them, gaining in intensity from city to city. It was better than any soap opera.

Besides everything else I was getting out of the trip, I was having a romance with a man who lived only ten blocks from me in New York City.

We swam in the Black Sea in Sochi, went to the beach by the Neva River in Leningrad, took midnight trolley rides, daytime boat trips, dined, and danced together.

I would say my opinion about tours changed at this point.

When I came home, I told everyone how terrific tours can be. I've been extolling their virtues ever since.

Another time I wanted to see the Amazon River, and I picked one called the "Green Hell" tour out of the travel section of *The New York Sunday Times*.

This one turned out a bit quirky, but it ended up being the second best vacation I ever had.

I bought my ticket and waited for the big day.

I couldn't think of anything more exciting than seeing the "Green Hell" of the jungle and the Amazon River.

I went to the airport thinking I'd see a big sign at the airline gate: "Green Hell" tour meets here. I didn't.

I got on the plane, sure that I would meet some other "Green Hell" travelers. I asked the person sitting next to me if he was going on the "Green Hell" trip. He looked startled, said no, and went back to reading his book.

I thought I might see people on the plane who had "Green Hell" buttons on their lapels; I was sure there had to be others going on this trip. So I searched up and down the aisles, but not a button popped up.

When I got off the plane in Bogota, Colombia, I thought *this* was where I'd find other people for the tour. Maybe they were all coming from different cities.

I was met by a tour guide at the airport. He shook hands and was very amiable. I asked him when I'd meet up with the other people who were on the "Green Hell" tour.

He said I was the only one who had signed up.

On the next leg of my Amazon trip, I talked to people on the plane who were taking the trip on their own. We joined forces and canoed all over the place, visited Indian tribes, walked over to Brazil (it took ten minutes), chopped our way through jungles, saw green lily pads the size of living room carpets, and went across the widest stretch of the Amazon in a putt-putt boat to Peru in the midst of the heaviest rainstorm I've ever encountered. We yelled and screamed and were in heaven.

I mention these mini-adventures to make the point of not overlooking trips that are part of tours.

I know one woman in her eighties living out on the West Coast who takes two or three tours a year: to see the changing fall leaves in New England; Mardi Gras in New Orleans; the Rose Bowl game in Pasadena. She says to her children as she sprints off, "I'm spending your inheritance!" And they love it.

WHEN

When to take a trip is simple: when you get itchy feet, when you have the time, and when you have the money. Many people have travel as one of their main interests, and it's what they're willing to save for. But with tours being as inexpensive as they are, travel is accessible to all income groups.

There is also another way to travel. Go someplace and live there for a while. I mentioned previously my wanderlust and traveling feet and living in various cities. I had a ball, learned a lot about life, about myself, other people, places, and about self-sufficiency and how not to be scared of any new situation that comes along.

The living and traveling situation can only happen if you don't have any obligations at the moment. In my case, I had worked my way through college, graduated, and thought, "I want to go see some things."

My parents were in good health, I had no children to care for, and only had to say goodbye to my college boyfriend (whom I had decided not to marry).

(I had even said good-bye to him once before, in the middle of college when I took one year off from school to work at Sun Valley, Idaho, where I did my famous skiing. Even at that time he thought I had too much wanderlust in me. I went wherever and whenever I wanted to.)

Within a week after graduating from college with my B.A. Degree in Business Administration (my mother said, "Take business, there will always be business going on in the world") I flew the coop and went to Los Angeles. A friend of our family worked for an airline there. I applied for a job, and got it. From the job I found two roommates, and I was on my way.

After two years of Los Angeles, I decided I wanted to go to London. However, London decided it didn't want an American to come there to work — it was a "Londoners only" basis if you lived there and worked.

I didn't want to spend time banging on foreign country's doors to get work permits, so I did what I thought was the next best thing, I moved to Honolulu with two chums. They moved back to the mainland in six months, and I stayed there two years — *every* day with 72 degree perfect weather. Do you know what it's like to wake up every day to 72 degree perfect weather? I stayed in Honolulu one and one-half years too long and should have come back in six months with the others. I got a job teaching English at a Business College, and I had a bee in my bonnet to work for a masters degree at the University of Hawaii, but I never completed it. I couldn't take the 72 degree perfect weather anymore. I lost interest in the Masters, and picked my next choice of cities.

San Francisco. The city is as beautiful as everyone who goes there says it is. However, I believe I stayed there four years longer than I should have. I saw all the sights in a few months, job pickings were not easy since they seemed to have a lot of branch offices for ad agencies and so forth, and there were more applicants for jobs in these small offices than there were jobs. The pickings on single men were not ample, either. All of the single women in the city moaned and groaned about it. We had a choice of either married men, alcoholic men, or homosexual men, and the latter group did not want us, anyway.

But, again, there were experiences in San Francisco I never would have had in any other city. It was there I learned that if you can't, as a person living alone, have a place to live in, that's the pits.

All I could afford there was the pits, and I never had a prosperous feeling about myself— mainly because I wasn't prosperous. The city just wasn't supplying me with fabulously-paid jobs.

In any city I lived in, I learned as much about myself as I did the city. So after five years of San Francisco and environs, I headed back from whence I started, New York, at the ripe old age of 30.

If circumstances allow, among all your other travel plans, go live in another city for a year or so. It may be one of the best most educational times you've ever had. With any luck, you'll enjoy a new job, new friends, new outlook. Pick a place where you may know someone, just to get started, and remember that saying, "A life without risk is nothing." It's an idea to think about.

WHERE

There are so many interesting places to go and see, I'll start you out with a simple list:

- Visit the penguins in Antarctica.
- Go to a resort hotel and sign up for a tennis improvement week.
- Go on a pub-exploration tour in London.
- Go see all the waterways and evergreen trees in Seattle.
- Watch a golf tournament in Pebble Beach.
- Go to Moscow in the winter or the summer or anytime.
- Go flying in a four-seater plane over Yellowstone Park.
- Go diving for treasure.
- Go people-watching in Barcelona.
- Visit Aunt Minnie in Cincinnati.
- Exchange your house for someone's in Paris for a month.
- Take a bed and breakfast trip through New England.
- Sign up for a bicycle tour.
- Go to Las Vegas or Reno and see what that's all about.
- Buy an Amtrak pass and tour the country.
- Take a trip on the Orient Express.
- Go to the opera in Vienna.
- Go on an expedition and see the great turtles, lizards, and iguanas in the Galapagos.
- Take a freighter trip for a month.
- Go to Tahiti and see what that's all about.
- Go to Australia and visit the koala bear in the ad and the man who says "G'day, Mate."

Has this list made your feet itch and your mouth water?

I hope so.

Traveling was made for the one-person householder. All we have to do is call the airline, pack a bag, turn out the lights, lock the door, and go.

Chart 27. A Sampling of Highs that Can Occur in Your Life

It's Chart Time.

Let's recount some of the good things you as a one-person householder get:

A SAMPLING OF HIGHS THAT CAN OCCUR IN YOUR LIFE

- You have no one in your household telling you that you *must* do something you don't want to do.
- You have more time for others than anyone living in any other type of household.
- You have more time for yourself than anyone living in any other type of household.
- You can luxuriate amongst fluffy pillows all day long.
- You can put household chores on the back burner.
- You can plan weekdays and weekends exactly as they suit you.
- You can be alone when you want to be alone.
- You can be with people whenever you want to be with people.
- The place where you live is yours to fix any way you want.
- Any and all interests you have can be pursued, for once and for all.
- You can get a feeling of family life by going to visit *families*.
- A romance is made in heaven at a one-person household.
- Vacations are simple to take — you call the airline and go.
- If you want to celebrate anything, you open up your house and celebrate on the spur of the moment.
- You don't know what or whom you'll meet around the next corner.
- You're free to follow any whim.
- A day is filled with more surprises than Heinz has varieties.
- You have the time, space, and energy to grow into the person you were meant to be.

28 Interviews. What Do Other People Think About People Living Alone?

The people below were picked at random to answer the question: "What do you think living alone is like?" The only thing they all had in common is that they either had not ever lived alone, or had lived alone only briefly in the distant past.

The people were all good sports. They knew only the title of my book and the general drift of it. So they answered "blind," not knowing how many plusses about living alone successfully had been laid out in all the chapters before this one.

They lived with their families when growing up, lived with roommates in college and after, got married, had kids, and had no periods of living alone. It was as though I was asking them what they think living on the moon was like. It simply was something they hadn't experienced and they could only use their imaginations and feelings as to what they thought it might be like.

I appreciate their honest responses. They added some interesting perspectives to the subject.

QUESTION: WHAT DO YOU THINK LIVING ALONE IS LIKE?
from L. L., English teacher, Annandale, VA:
"First, I'm married. And when you're married or living with someone, there's a lot of discipline imposed on your life. It's an education. You should get an advanced degree or a bronze plaque. You've managed to live with the most impossible person in the world, and if you add children, the next most impossible ones.

"Can this be good? Yes, for you've probed the mystery of unmatched socks and you've thought up meals not to offend the palate of Mr. Gourmet. And you've tolerated symphonic music so loud the orchestra might be right there in your ears. But these domestic rites make the joyous pulse beat of life together.

"If I lived alone, this is how I imagine I would live. I'd have a house that looked always like an unmade bed. I'd eat meals limited to a single dish, like Shrimp Newburg, because the lettuce wilted to swamp grass, the tomatoes grew mold, the stale bread could double for floor tiles, and there's never dessert because of the calories.

"The door of the liquor cabinet would never rust on its hinges. A proper meal needs the gracious prelude of a cocktail. The warmed-over entree needs to be washed down with wine, and through the long evening, the boob tube's inanity and the boring bestseller needs the anesthesia of a stiff drink.

"Then I'd become a magazine junkie. (No self-respecting spouse would let that trashy reading into the house. Oh, how those slick monthlies make one swim in guilt when married.)

"My nail polish would probably be the wrong color, my hemline last year's, my apartment decor Salvation Army thriftshop.

"I'm sure people living alone also get hooked on phobias. Without a Saturday night date, one is as good as dead. Married homemakers are driven by things they gotta get done. On Saturday night one might be doing two washloads, cleaning the long neglected oven, editing out run-on sentences in a teenager's book report.

"And clothes would be a boa constrictor that chokes people living alone penniless. The live-aloners, when not eating over the sink, anguish ceaselessly about what's in and what's imminently out, while Mom with her brood is content in ten year old jeans and her husband's collar-frayed cast-off shirt. She may drag a vintage polyester from the closet for special occasions.

"But do your own thing. Don't be browbeaten by those togetherness disciples. Don't let them tear the twigs from the cozy nest you are in.

"What more can I say — to each his own, or 'Chacun a son gout,' as the French say.

"And I wouldn't be a bit surprised if *your* place has signed etchings, Breuer chairs, Anne Klein and Ralph Lauren clothes, purebred dogs or cats, and Chicken Kiev on its Limoges plate, chilled Moselle in its Waterford glass, and the sterling gleaming on the table."

E. G. H., Junior High School Clerical Aide, Tacoma, WA:

"I would have to say it's probably a *very* solitary existence, and a person living alone would have to become very independent.

"There are no time schedules to keep in the home. One could do wash at eleven o'clock at night, leave the bed unmade, and hang dripping clothes on the towel rack in the bathroom.

"But when you're married, as I am, you know the house has to be kept in order, because neighbors, children, and in-laws all drop in unannounced.

"It seems to me that when one lives alone, life is programmed.

"And eating habits would be different, because you don't need to cook large amounts and you'd eat foods that please only you. When you're married, you tend to cook for the other person — or I should say, you cook to please both parties, not just yourself.

"Another thing. If you're living alone and are a woman and have a car, you have to rely on professional mechanics to take care of it. If you're married, your husband will know when things are going wrong with it and will fix it.

"I think living alone means it's hard to find a compatible partner to share sports activities. Say on a Sunday I wanted to play golf, and I lived alone. Would I be able to find another person who shared the same interest in playing that Sunday?

"I can't really imagine what it would be like to live alone, as I've never done it in my entire life. But the main drawback to me is you get lonesome and don't have somebody there to talk to.

"When people live alone, they have to do all the planning ahead for their lives and they can't expect that someone else's income will help them out. There's a big financial factor in living alone.

"The first thought that would ever come to me if I lived alone would be: how will I handle my financial matters? Next, I know I'd have to get a better job to get more money coming in, and then I'd have to get back into circulation socially.

"I could handle it. But it sure wouldn't be easy."

E. B., Attorney, Dallas, TX:

"I don't see why anyone would ever want to live alone. I don't know how they can stand not having anyone around, it must be the loneliest thing I can think of not to have anyone there when you walk in the door.

"And then you have to eat alone, too. All I can picture is a person sitting there hour after hour with no one there.

"I have to have some people around me, or at least ONE person who I know is right there.

"I don't even need to have my wife in the same room with me, but I have to know she's *somewhere* in the house, then I feel everything's all right. I can go on with my reading or whatever else I'm doing as long as I know she's there.

"If something happened where I found myself living alone, I'd get married or hooked up to someone again, because I definitely wouldn't want to be left alone."

C. W., Sales Rep, New York, NY:

"I was divorced two years ago, but right away I started sharing an apartment with a guy some friends said was looking for a roommate to help pay the rent.

"I didn't want to go live alone, that's for sure. I can't live alone.

"This guy I'm sharing the apartment with really gets on my nerves, he's such a dunce. But at least I'm not living alone.

"I mostly go out to dinner and to the bars in the neighborhood after work and do my socializing there, so I don't have to be with him that much.

"Just the thought of coming home to an empty place scares me. I don't know why. I guess because it's something I've never done, it just seems unthinkable. To me, it's a totally unacceptable way to live.

"But that's just me. I don't knock people who live alone, I give them a lot of credit."

G. E. C., Homemaker/Teacher/Artist, Briarcliff Manor, NY:

"I'm married, and have been for a long time, and have a big family, but when I think about what it must be like to live alone, these are the things that come to mind:
- Be able to skip meals, eat what I like, hot or cold, on a table or tray, or while dashing.
- Be able to always to pick up the mail first.
- Wouldn't have to turn down the volume of an opera.
- Be able to cook franks and sauerkraut at midnight without complaints about the smell.
- There'd be no competition for the Sunday *Times* crossword

puzzle.
- Be able to open and close windows when my temperature dictated.
- Dine out often.
- Be able to wear socks to bed when needed.
- Be able to rise early or late or not go to bed at all.
- Be able to let the wash, ironing, and dishes pile high.
- Have absolute peace and quiet with no commitments to fill.

"These are the disadvantages that I think are in the lifestyle of living alone:
- Lack of companionship and someone to care for and worry about.
- No one there for emergencies or when you're ill.
- No one to give you a push and the urge to complete necessary tasks.
- No one to share a meal with.
- No one awaiting your arrival home.
- No one to argue with.
- No one to love at home.

"The good things about living alone are fun to dream about, but I wouldn't change much from the way I have it now."

29
Interviews. What do One-Person Householders Think About Living Alone

The people interviewed here were fairly used to living alone, and they appreciated being able to tell what they thought were the good parts and the not-so-nifty stuff. It seemed to average out to eighty percent good things in a one-person household living arrangement, and twenty percent of things that happen — or not — that they didn't like.

By coincidence, this overall perception is what I was aiming for in Chapter 1.

Thirteen people interviewed does not constitute a scientific sample, but their opinions do make the 80 / 20 percents interesting to think about. These people were free to say anthing they wanted about their lifestyle, no holds barred. Here's what they said.

QUESTION: WHAT DO YOU THINK ABOUT LIVING ALONE?

R.S., Graphic Artist, New York, NY:

"The *best* thing is that I can do anything I want, whenever I want, at any time of the day or night, and there's no one there to ask me why. I can spontaneously change my mind without having someone to answer to. For example, I'd say, 'I've decided to go out running,' and there's no one there to say, 'But I thought you said you were going to sleep.'

"Another good thing which seems to be very important to me is that I can eat whenever, wherever, and whatever I want to in my apartment.

"Also, there are no distractions to interrupt my concentration, unless I allow them to be there.

"The main disadvantage is that there isn't someone there when

167

I want to share something wonderful I've done that day, or that I've seen — or even someone to hold when I'm crying because there's been a disappointment.

"I handle that by calling a friend, going to his or her place, and getting what I need in the way of comfort and understanding, then going home. It all works out very well.

"I must say that ninety percent of the time I'm glad no one else is at my place, however.

"I've honestly always thought that I would like to have a very loving, supportive relationship, but each of us would have our *own* place to live — so that we could live together sometimes, but we didn't HAVE TO all the time. That would solve it for me."

L.D., Clarinetist, New York, NY:

"When I'm alone I can do what I want on my own schedule. I can sleep late if I want or if I want to go to bed at 4:00 A.M. it won't bother anyone.

"I can practice my clarinet any time of the day or night. If I was living with someone, this would drive them up the wall.

"I have all this freedom to do what I want to do without worrying about someone else being ticked off by it.

"By the same token, I miss the companionship of a female — but when I start thinking about it I'm reminded about the tremendous pressure of breaking up, making up, trying to keep that someone pleased and happy. But who knows, there's always hope.

"The pressure of preparing for a musical performance is a different type of pressure — a good pressure.

"I have a lot of people around me and have camaraderie and friendships that are beneficial and constructive, and it's enjoyable. My friends are supportive, constructive, and 'with me.'

"And the guys in my group, I dig every one of them, that's why we're together. They're right there when I need them for gigs in and around New York City.

"People who feel that they have to be with someone because they can't stand to be alone — and not really enjoying that person's company or being with them — that's really pathetic. Being with someone without enjoyment just so you won't have to be alone is a terrible way to live. I'm glad I can bypass that way of living."

R.F., Screenwriter/University Professor, New York, NY:

"I like the freedom of space and movement and time so that my schedule is controlled by my own dictates and desires.

"If I want to write a letter at three o'clock in the morning, I won't be waking somebody with my typewriter. Or if I want to go for a walk or eat at any hour, I just get up and do it.

"I like the feeling of being able to control 100 percent of the environment around me, because I can't do that on the outside, for example, people, bus services, dirt. But here I can regulate the 'temperature' of my existence.

"One thing I dislike about living alone is that packaged food and all sorts of items in the stores are for 'plurals.' It means that a lot of times you have to buy much more than you can use or eat.

"I also realize that my feelings of cooking and eating are *social* feelings — to 'eat with someone.' And I find I more than likely will simply do nothing for myself as far as eating well is concerned. I find it funny to make a big meal and then sit down and serve it to myself. Maybe I'm not schizophrenic enough to make my other personality serve me?

"When I go a long time without being with someone else, it turns out to be a disadvantage. It gets to a point that it would be helpful, productive, and very nice to hear an opinion different from my own once in a while.

"But I think living alone you experience and feel deep inside what it means to be alone. And it makes you appreciate much more other people's independence — in the same way you respect and value your own."

S. B., Arts Classicist, New York, NY:

"Most people would rather be living with someone they care for, or at least like a lot, and I'm one of them. But since living alone is the circumstance I've found myself in, let me tell you the pluses of being a single-householder.

"First, there's the delicious freedom of indulging my whims:

- I can choose to go right home after work or stay out.
- Be as neat as a pin around the house, or as sloppy as my aesthetic sense will allow.
- Dine on haute cuisine or slap together a peanut butter and jam sandwich.
- Be totally alone when I don't feel like talking, or else seek company.
- Dress to the teeth, or shlump around in baggy pants.
- Plan a lovely weekend with friends, or go comatose for the

weekend.

"All this I can do without having to account to anyone else for my actions.

"Another advantage is that I don't get stalemated in this lifestyle.

"I'm always making new friends, taking up new interests — and there's no worry as to whether or not it may annoy another person in my household.

"Now, while all the above is great stuff, let's face it — there's still no substitute for the warmth of a happily shared domicile. I'd allow an expansion of my single abode if the addition made giving up my cherished whims seem a small price to pay.

"In the meantime...I think I'll save that nutritious food I bought for tonight's dinner in the refrig...and ecstasize on ice cream for dinner instead!"

H. W. S., Editor, Charlottesville, VA:

"I'm married now and have a two year old daughter, but before my marriage, I loved living alone — and sometimes it stills looks pretty good. But I don't have any plans to change my situation at the moment.

"One of the best things about living alone was being able to eat whatever I wanted whenever I wanted, and I didn't have to 'stash' and 'hide' food as I do now. I'm a chocoholic and ashamed of it. I hide chocolate now so that either it doesn't get eaten before I get to it, or so no one else knows I have it. (I can go through a pound of M&M's without my husband even knowing I've had it in the house.)

"Another great thing is the amount of *time* that you have living alone that isn't available when you're sharing your living space.

"I loved the time to do what *I* wanted to do, whether it was painting a room, painting a picture, or doing nothing. I love to read, and it seems I never have enough time to do all the reading that I'd like to do now that I'm married.

"Another thing (and this just occurred to me as I looked at my living room), if you're living alone and your place is a mess, it's your mess, and no one else's. And if it's clean, it will stay that way until *you* mess it up.

"The downside of living alone was fear, either that somebody quirky would be standing outside watching my apartment (which happened once), or having an emergency get out of control (which happened twice).

"Once I put my arm through a window trying to close it, and there was no one home in my building, probably for the first time in history. Since I had cut my right hand and had a standard shift car, I couldn't drive myself to the hospital. Bleeding like a stuck pig, I ran across the street to the only house with lights on, and pounded on the door with my left hand, dripping blood all over the guy's porch. The man who answered the door then drove me to the hospital.

"I have an inner ear problem which is characterized by the room spinning around and terrible nausea. The first time it happened I lay on the kitchen floor wondering how to get some help. I couldn't move. My apartment had ten steps leading from the front door up to the actual apartment and I had put the chain up on the front door. So even if I could get to the telephone to phone someone, I couldn't go down the steps to open the chain to let them in!

"Another thing I found a disadvantage of living alone was Sundays. I hated Sundays. I've read that this is rather common, and I don't know why it is — whether there are fewer things available to do on Sundays, or what; it always seemed a very bleak day. Especially around four o'clock in the afternoon. Nothing had happened so far, and nothing was going to happen. And there was only golf on TV, and I hate golf.

"But I must say that about ninety percent of the time, in the long run, I did enjoy living by myself before I got married."

L. G. B., Master of Library Science, New York, NY:

"I think living alone is a great experience.

"Here at my home, I can be myself. I can talk to myself, to my plants, to the pictures on the wall, and there's no one to criticize me or raise an eyebrow or make me feel like a weirdo.

"I can stay in bed on Saturday morning with remote control TV and flick stations with one eye closed if I feel like it.

"I say, you can always live with someone, but living alone takes PLANNING to do well. But it's definitely worth it.

"The things I like the most are: I can come and go as I please; I don't have to clean or cook if I don't want to.

"The one thing I don't like is if I need a person and I'm alone, it can be very frustrating. It's good to have a shoulder right there to cry on or to talk to. But this doesn't happen often.

"And in times of need I can always visit someone, or call someone. Even when the hot water isn't running in my building, I can visit a friend and take a bath there!

"All in all, I like living alone."

J. S., Assistant to Corporate Vice President, Fashion Industry, New York, NY:

"What I like most about my 'state of one' is my freedom to make choices. When I step outside my apartment door I can fill up my time with as many activities or obligations as I want. When I step back inside and close the door, there's just me to entertain. And I'm good company.

"I can tub-soak until my skin wrinkles. And on rainy Sundays — love 'em! I can be as lazy or creative as my mood dictates. What and how much I eat depends solely on my degree of success with recipes.

"I live alone, but I'm not alone. There's always some project in the works. For instance, since there aren't any shopping malls in Manhattan — and I'm a shopping mall freak — when one opens up in New Jersey or in one of the boroughs, my friend Pat and I will go tootlin' off in her own construction company's truck to see it. And I can call her at the drop of a hat and we just go.

"I don't believe I ever thought I'd be living alone. I was always so busy and involved with the 'day at hand,' and I guess I just assumed that someday I'd have the big country house, lots of greenery (to mow and spend), and a few kids.

"But let's bring these facts into perspective: I have a cozy studio apartment in midtown Manhattan, a few healthy, burgeoning green plants, and a bank balance that squeaks.

"Living alone is a tricky business. It makes you look inside yourself — and sometimes you have to 'clean closets' and regroup.

"You start by being your own best friend, and the rest is easy.

"Do I wish for someone to share my life with? Of course I do.

"I keep my mind always receptive to new ideas and challenges. And when I think my spirit is turning chicken, I high-tail it into the kitchen where on the cupboard door is a small newspaper clipping, yellowed with age.

"It's a short quote by Alan Alda included in his commencement address to one of his daughter's graduating classes. Here it is:

" 'Have the nerve to go into unexpected territory. Be brave

enough to live creatively. Leave the city of your comfort and go into the wilderness of your intuition. What you will discover will be wonderful. What you'll discover is yourself.'

"I like living alone — until something better comes along."

B.A., Banker, New York, NY:

"I'm satisfied living alone. It's difficult for me to compare it to being married, because I've never been married, and living alone has been my natural state.

"I can do my own chores, it's no big deal. If anyone wants to come and volunteer to do my chores for me, that's fine too. But I can handle things that have to be done.

"I like to eat out or have someone over and we cook together, so I find the eating proposition of living alone no problem.

"The drawback, of course, is that you don't have someone around to talk to exactly at the moment you want someone, or someone to rely on, or someone to just be there when you'd like it.

"Things generally are pretty good, and who knows what or *who*, is around the corner waiting for me.

R.T., Freelance Writer, NYC:

"Unless one is an eremite-in-training, living alone is as unnatural as dyeing one's hair. But in the reality of the 80's, we all may do it at one time or another.

"My learning to live on my own began when I finally faced up to the fact that single life might not be a temporary apparition to be stoically endured when I was between marriages.

"After ten years of living alone, I think I've turned it into an art form. No longer does my apartment look like a temporary shelter surrounded by crates. I've made my surroundings reflect my taste and cater to my senses. I like my home.

"I cherish certain items. I treasure my books and my paintings. They're not first editions or Rembrandts, but they're mine and I enjoy them.

"But most of all, because I hate being lonely, I refuse to 'live alone.' I share my life and my home with two Siamese cats. They are both big-mouthed opinionated communicators who let me know the instant I stray from acceptable human behavior. They demand my attention and my love. They greet me with delight when I come home, and censure me with mournful looks when I leave. They shower me with purring, and it seems when I feel most alone, there they are, and as if by magic, I feel better, even cossetted. Like me, they enjoy their own privacies, and we respect each other's moods. Our relationship is almost parasitic— I need them much more than they need me.

"And I keep connected to a whole range of people who come in for dinner, a drink, or brunch. People who enjoy my company at a concert, a movie, or a play.

"To them I can freely communicate my hopes and successes, my fears and my failures. Like my cats, my friends accept me — warts and all— so I consider that my single apartment is full of life, full of love, full of deep satisfaction and soaring pleasures — not the least of which are the men who occasionally share my daily existence. I'm grateful for every facet of my present life.

"Living alone need not mean living lonely...I've proved it."

R.B., Development Consultant, New York, NY:
"You come into the world alone, and you go out of the world alone.

"And in between you have a wonderful opportunity NOT to be alone, and I feel that *living* alone doesn't necessary mean that you *are* alone.

"As human beings we have the ability and the need to love other people. As we all know, there many types of loves — for friends, relatives, husbands, boyfriends.

"The important thing in having a fulfilling life, whether you live alone or not, is to know who *you* are. As you grow in that knowledge, you can share your life in so many ways with so many people. Living alone can be turned into a joyous experience.

"There are also times of sadness, of wanting to have someone there immediately to share a problem. There's also the wanting of closeness of family ties and feeling needed or wanted. But from what I've heard, this also happens when people live together.

"In the long run, we were never promised a rose garden, and we just have to learn to continue the journey, share, and grow.

"And in doing so, we create quality for ourselves and for the other people in our lives."

P.S., Freelance Writer-Producer, New York, NY:
"I grew up in a loving family environment, also enjoyed dorm living at school, living in a 'Y', and renting a room in a friend's house.

I shared a long-time weekend relationship with a very special man, and I've raised a nephew who's very important to me.

"Yet my greatest growing experience has been living alone. I relish it — the independence of it, the constant challenge of being completely responsible for one's own life.

"Even in childhood I sought lots of time alone.

"It refreshes my mind and soul and makes my time with those I love more meaningful.

"Besides this, three great things about living alone are:
- I can walk naked around my spacious apartment.
- I can eat cold pizza for breakfast.
- I can read and write all through the night.

"I have what I *want* right now. I'm living alone, but not lonely."

N.M., Actress, Los Angeles, CA:

"1. It's all you. Everything's self-generated, the pleasure and the pain. There's no one to blame or take the credit for the good times and the bad.

"2. There's plenty of time for self-exploration, meditation, and introspection.

"3. It's your nest with no compromises."

M.S., Author and Teacher, Tacoma, WA:

"Enjoying the 'single life' is more a mental attitude than a physical state. I use the quotes as I never think of myself as single — as opposed to married — any more than I think of myself as sixty — as opposed to being fifty or forty or thirty.

"Instead, I think of myself as a fortunate, capable, independent woman, possessing the health, wealth, and intellect to pursue two rewarding careers.

"For thirty-two years I was a dependent wife and mother of six children, with a frustrating inferiority complex that threatened to keep me housebound for the rest of my life (and I hate housework). One fateful day I read a review of Martin Heidegger's philosophy in *Newsweek.* He said something like, 'Most people lead their lives of quiet desperation and never achieve the strength of will to change.'

"Suddenly I felt all the contrariness my mother had always accused me of as a child surge through me like an incoming riptide. (I was living in a waterfront home on an island with a thirty-foot yacht moored in a lagoon behind the house.)

"I immediately took my eight year old son and my twenty year old son and moved out.

"I learned to rely on the advice of professionals for handling the business and 'man-oriented' affairs I had always left up to my husband. I had my first checking account ever — at age forty-eight.

"Since that moment I've been a truly happy person. The world became a fascinating place full of exciting, interesting individuals.

"I experience a phenomenal rebirth with all the drive and curiosity of a teenager. I started writing books with a confidence I'd never had before.

"Today with my eleventh book in the works and the support and companionship of my newfound colleagues, who could ask for anything more?

"I have all the men I need. I certainly do enjoy men a lot more. Because I was resenting the hold my husband had over me, it made me resent all men before my lifestyle changed.

"I have all sorts of people around me — grandchildren, kids, in-laws, an extended family of twenty-five people.

"So even though I live alone, I never feel alone.

"The one stupid thing that I really enjoy the most is going on a shopping spree to the mall and coming home and putting it *out* and displaying it on my living room couch instead of wrapping it up and hiding it under my bed. (I used to have to hide it, because my husband didn't want me to spend any money.)

"I think women are far more suited to living alone than men because of the way men are raised — to expect someone to take care of all their chores and all their needs.

"I teach elementary school, as well as write and get novels published. I'll never give up teaching, because it keeps me in touch with the world. I have to know the slang terms, the way people are thinking. I need to be in touch with young people in order to keep my writing fresh, and I love those kids in my sixth grade class.

"I've always thought that your home should reflect you and your personality, and my first home never did. I hated everything in it. Now I've got a collection of 3,000 books, and everything in my home reflects me. I look at it and feel 'at home'.

"My ideal kitchen, by the way, is one that has no stove, no sink, no cupboards. Just a telephone (to call for dinner reservations and fast food) and a chaise longue to lie on while making the calls."

Congratulations. You're Living Alone Successfully, Not Eating Over the Sink, and Having a Fantastic Life

30

Most people quoted in the last chapter went on at length on what they like about living alone, and gave a sentence or two about the pits.

(And I didn't even have to give each of them $5 to talk like that.)

There seems to be something comforting about our lifestyle — we're amazingly content, as long as we figure out *how* to do it.

By using the household and non-household hints in this book, I believe you can get at least an 80% yum/20% crumb ratio going in your life.

There could even be things you already do that make for an improved live-alone life that I haven't thought of. You have an even better ratio of yums to crumbs. That's great.

Now let's go.

Let's see how you, the one-person householder, can be living:

● You have your money situation in fairly good shape, your time somewhat planned, household chores and emergencies reduced, and you haven't turned funny from staying alone too long.

● You've adjusted your weekdays, weekends, food, and sleep habits to perfection, and you hardly ever eat over the sink.

● You see your friends when you want to and you have a pet that adores you (if you want to have a pet).

● Your seams are sewn together properly and you catch them as they burst.

● The place where you live is to your liking.

● You're doing everything you've ever wanted to do, you're giving and going to social events that suit you, and you're mingling

with all sorts of people. You're making good things happen for yourself and other people.
- You're improving the situations in the areas of romance, the blahs, and the holidays.
- And you celebrate your birthday because you're glad you were born and are having an interesting life.
- You're to be congratulated. You're living alone successfully!

Index

179

About the Author

Edan Schappert is in the middle of enjoying a productive and successful career with *Newsweek Magazine*. However, that statement of fact describes only the workday life of this talented New Yorker. A member of the Author's Guild and the Dramatists Guild, among others, she has had four radio scripts (comedies) produced by the corporation for Public Broadcasting and thirteen plays produced in New York and Boston. In addition, she won the Northwestern University Nationwide Script Competition.

Although *The Sophisticate's Guide to Living Alone Successfully* is her first book, she has – in addition to her script and playwriting – had her work published in *The Dramatists Guild Quarterly* and *The Humanitarian Magazine*.

Edan lives in Manhattan's East Side, in an older apartment building that offers an unusual midtown amenity . . . a terrace with trees!